Black Tea

Stephen Morris

CLARET PRESS

Copyright © Stephen Morris 2019
The moral right of the author has been asserted.

ISBN paperback: 978-1-910461-38-9
ISBN ebook: 978-1-910461-39-6

A CIP catalogue record for this book is available from the British Library.

This paperback can be ordered from all bookstores as well as from Amazon, and the ebook is available on online platforms such as Amazon and iBooks.

Cover and Interior Design by Petya Tsankova

www.claretpress.com

PROLOGUE

Ovid was exiled to the Black Sea port of Tomis at the end of his life for reasons that have never been fully understood. All through his long journey from Rome he began what was to be his final work, a series of books that make up the melancholic, complaining Tristia *and* Ex Ponto. *On his arrival he was given a helmet and a spear and told to help fight barbarians, wild men with icicles tinkling in their beards who wore skins and came from that place which is now called Russia. His knees shook, he dropped his spear. Afterwards, he locked himself in his room and wrote long, ever more despairing letters pleading for his return.*

Some of the letters he burnt. Those that were sent on to Rome and still survive, talk of a country located at the far ends of the earth, and of a dread of being crushed by its soil after death. He fell ill, and in his nightmares he saw the Russian-barbarians rounding up those innocents who hadn't yet been taken, putting them in chains, setting fire to their hovels, and communicating in a language that sounded like the harsh screaming of animals.

It's difficult to distinguish between his poetry (miserable, touching) and the real effort he was engaged in to rally others around his cause, but by the end it becomes clear he is writing for himself, even perhaps with no thought of being read. Grey, still trembling, he eked out his final months thinking of his beloved, bringing her to life in her absence more fully than he had ever done before, opening his heart without shame. He died alone, ununited, unpardoned, unreconciled.

SUMMER

1

For a time Russia meant simply somewhere cold. Beyond this thought were details: a fur hat, troikas speeding across the snow, bearded men in peasant smocks pulling on a barge – the Volga Boatmen – their heads bowed in physical effort, and also in a spiritual struggle. I began to wonder how it might feel to be enslaved, but this didn't put me off. It seemed that one day, somehow or other, I would go there, and that this business would keep me occupied for a good while.

On the hall table in the house where I grew up was a lacquered box painted with three horses rearing on thin legs, their long necks and muscular bodies straining with human eroticism. A factory name was printed across the base in odd rounded-out letters, an unpronounceable word that began with a P and ended with a long number, a slash, and then a dot. I could just reach to pull it towards me if I stretched on tip-toe and then, sitting on the bottom stair with the box in my lap, I took a look inside. It was empty, with dust gathering in the corners, but I didn't want to let it go and ran my fingers across the polished top, over the orange and yellow forms of the horses and their jeweled harnesses, and over the velvet-black background that signified something remote and deep, like a night without an end.

Every so often, though probably much less frequently than it seems to me now, my father brought home toys from the Russian shop on Holborn. He chose them because they were nicely made of wood and had been produced in a Communist country, and because he felt he was helping the Socialist cause. I think he also liked them because they were cheap. Sometimes he brought books from the same shop, Russian fairy stories published by the Raduga press, with big papery pages and outlandish pictures. One of my favourite books from this time was an old hard-backed edition of Baron

Munchausen's adventures in Russia. I would get myself comfortable and read of that far-away place, of how the Baron crossed an endless snow plain where there were no people, no buildings, not even any trees. He tied his horse to a stump, worn out after a day of adventures, and fell into a deep sleep using his saddle as a pillow. In the morning he woke up in the middle of a village. There was a loud neighing, and to his astonishment he saw his horse hanging from a church roof. What he had taken for a stump the previous evening had been a weathervane poking through the snow. During the night the snow had melted and the intrepid Baron had sunk all the way to street level, while his horse had remained stuck at the top of the church.

Much later, when I was beginning to find my own way in life, after many hesitations and delays, I arrived in Moscow for the first time to find a country on the move. I had travelled from England where the newspapers were talking of AIDS. They had done so before, but now the situation was worse and the story wouldn't go away. Hirohito, the Emperor of Japan, had died of cancer, and obituaries showed him dressed like any normal guy in a suit and tie. A fatwa raised against Salman Rushdie for writing and publishing *The Satanic Verses* was followed almost immediately by book burnings in Bradford. George Bush senior was elected president in America, comfortably beating the nicer-looking Michael Dukakis. The news could be explained away, but the fear of AIDS had begun to affect everyone like a psychosis, and it was confusing and there was no right way to think of it.

In Moscow I forgot all of this very quickly. On the streets and along station platforms and at bus terminals, people marched resolutely, struggling under the weight of bulging bags. The bags were dark and nondescript, like the clothes people wore. They often looked heavy and unmanageable, and in the crowd there was a determination I had never seen before. When you stepped onto a trolleybus or tram you were caught straight away in a scrum, not only of bodies but also of bags. The bags rested on the floor between everybody's legs, or they hung at awkward ankle-height, or they were clutched protectively with arms wrapped all around in a chest-high position and used like a brace, or sometimes in the last resort as a battering ram.

I had left my English life behind me and found something new. The novelty lasted but over the following months it became clear that trouble was on its way. You could feel it in the air, like a change in the weather. The system was falling apart, and everywhere you went people said the same thing, that their country was just the kind of place where you could never be sure what was going to turn up next and surprise you. They were quite firm on this point.

It was during this time, when I travelled frequently between Russia and England, that I got married. The ceremony was held in the small Buckinghamshire town of Beaconsfield, just down the road from the barracks where Muammar Gaddafi trained as an officer with the British army. Lyuba had lived all her life in Moscow. She was a graduate from the metallurgical institute on Leninsky Prospekt and with her tall figure, dark eyes, and pale skin, she was strikingly beautiful in a way that made people stop and stare on the street. I was always having to cope with admirers, either young men full of bravado, or older men who became bold and reckless, and ready to drop everything as if their lives depended on it.

She enjoyed making clothes, and had plastic bags full of folded Burda patterns traced on thin paper and stuffed into envelopes with instructions and coloured sketches of the finished items as they would look. Before our wedding she bought material from an old-fashioned haberdashery and made a red dress with cleverly designed folds that were supposed to conceal the fact she was pregnant. After we had signed the register and been congratulated by the usher, we stepped outside and posed next to our rust-spotted Volkswagen Polo while somebody took photographs. It was February, and a cold east wind gusting unpredictably through the carpark blew her thick dark hair to one side, and flattened the carefully constructed folds to reveal the obvious bump, couched in the tucks of satin like a giant Easter egg.

Our first child was born in Watford General hospital on a sunny April morning and shortly afterwards we moved to London, to a dark, damp flat that soon became known as an easy-going place where you would get fed and invited to stay over for as long as you might need. More and more Russians were taking advantage of the open-border policies, and in those first years we always had visitors, often with problems. Russians came and went until I lost count of them. They were directed to us by Lyuba's mother in Moscow, and they came to see Lyuba, but in the end they always turned to me, looking for answers to the sort of practical questions they felt an English person should know. There were all kinds of people: chancers looking for work on building sites, scientists applying for university funding, business people, a whole bunch of musicians, a factory owner, children left to fend for themselves in expensive public schools. I remember a convention of bridge champions, a lone round-the-world cyclist, orthodox Jews. We had criminal types. Sometimes we saw more of one sort than another, but for a while they arrived pretty steadily. Some were friends but most weren't.

Lyuba had brought her old samovar from Russia with its tin stove-pipe, and she set it up on the terrace on Sunday afternoons after boozy lunches, first filling it with water and then lighting the fire from the top with pine cones. I had learnt Russian with a book and a cassette, and the conversation swayed between Russian and English. Sometimes English words were mixed into the Russian, not for my benefit but to express something particularly English, or just to convey that one was talking in England, and of England, from a Russian point of view. While we talked a dense white smoke moved through the back gardens, smothering the yellow acacias and the lower branches of a lime tree that spread over our shed. When the water was boiled we pushed the hot pipe off with a stick and brought the samovar back in, clearing a space on the table with a saucer under the tap to catch the drips, and a pot of strong tea nearby for the refills and the top-ups. The tea drinking went with the cake eating, and there was something life-giving about both the tea and the cake after the vodka drinking that continued all through lunch with bottles still frosted from the freezer, and toasts that kept coming even when there was nothing left to say.

With the Russians came Russian food shops, Russian language newspapers, and headlines connected to the new Russian rich and their world of corrupt business. There were stories of sensational shootings, of shady deals with western involvement that always went wrong in the lobbies of upmarket hotels, or on the street in clear daylight outside new car dealerships, or in the subterranean murk of Moscow night clubs. Soon it became clear that this was only a fraction of the goings-on, the tip of the iceberg of criminality, and that all over Russia turf wars were being fought over the right to conduct business and over who owned what. A lid had been lifted on a whole lot of rottenness, and greed was spilling out everywhere at once.

After Yeltsin stepped down, in 1999, the Russian government declared war against the oligarchs, a year-on-year attack prosecuted with simple ruthlessness by the security forces and the judiciary. The most sensational of the actions reported in the English newspapers involved the murder of Alexander Litvinenko, a former FSB agent who had moved to London and begun speaking out against the organisation he once worked for. Litvinenko was slipped a dose of polonium in a quiet bar in the Millennium hotel on Grosvenor Square, and a few hours later he woke in his apartment with terrible stomach pains. He spent three weeks in a London hospital, dying slowly and agonizingly. The papers ran a picture of him just before the end, his flesh wasted away, his hair fallen out, and his arms stretched claw-like, following the direction of his sunken stare. He looked like Rembrandt's famous painting of Lazarus rising corpse-like from the dead, and afterwards, when it became known that he had died from polonium poisoning and that suspicion fell on the Kremlin, there was outrage. David Cameron invoked an image of old England, upholding the ancient rights of liberty and the rule of law. Russia went quiet for a while and people wondered whether this might not prove to be a watershed moment.

But it turned out that Russia didn't need England with its ancient rights and rules. Beyond crime and corruption lay a different concept of value, more absolute and more mystical than England's. It was not that a person meant less in Russia, rather that a person's worth was not measured necessarily by his living life, or his living freedom.

It was around this time that I joined a Sunday morning

swimming club in the pool near to where we lived in Herne Hill. I remember sharing a lane with a balding, grizzled man. He was one of the eight o'clock regulars, and half way through the session we both rested for a while in the shallow end with our arms on the side, getting our breath back. He asked me if I was going away for the holidays, and I told him that I was leaving for Russia the following week. 'Russia!' he said, almost choking with surprise. Then he began explaining how nothing had changed in that country, how it was as bad as ever, and how the state couldn't bring itself to stop terrorizing its own people. I listened over the screams and splashes with my goggles pressed tightly against my forehead, wondering how this middle-aged Englishman, clearly exhausted after pushing himself so hard with his front crawl, had managed to find time to form so complete an opinion.

Sometime later I came across Marusz Wilk's book in which he quotes from Tyutchev, the poet who wrote that Russia could only be believed in, that it could not be understood. Wilk went on to say that he wanted, as a true agnostic, to substitute Tyutchev's word, *belief*, for experience. He wanted to experience Russia in order to satisfy himself that it existed.

I didn't need to satisfy myself that Russia existed. I already had my family: my wife and children and my in-laws, both in Russia and in London, and their friends and acquaintances, a whole solid set of people all with their own lives and their own ideas of how things were. But for the time being Russia was still something people felt bound either to support or condemn. The man with the grey complexion who used to push himself so hard in the swimming pool had shared his opinion in the same way, or so it seemed to me, as those English people in the seventies who raised their hands in horror after reading *The Gulag Archipelago* and decided, without questioning their own commitment, that enough was enough. It was the same instinct that had stirred the souls of Victorian adventurers to help black Africans rid themselves of witches and demons, and it bothered me to rebel. It was a rebellion against certainty in the defence of principles, which had violence at its root and which I had encountered many times before in otherwise considerate people.

I felt like Hemingway when he saw a bone sticking out of a matador, and noted the hard whiteness and the soiled undergarments in the dust of the bull ring. Their certainty was like that bone, pushing through the warm flesh when it shouldn't have been there at all.

2

The voice at the end of the line is harsh but also faint. The harshness has an edge to it like rough, dark wine. The faintness might have something to do with the reception, which is poor where I am in this small corner of Suffolk, not far from the North Sea coast. Or it could be that Lyuba has already left Moscow and is in Vashutino, the village where she visits her parents every summer. To get a good signal in Vashutino you have to walk to the end of the village, past the rubbish bins where the land opens up, and before the forest starts. It's unlikely she would have done that.

'Well? Did you get it?'

It sounds like she's shouting, but still I can hardly hear.

'It's here! I picked it up myself. Yes...I got it!'

Now I'm shouting, but I can't tell whether she's understood. There's a silence, then some gurgling sounds, and the line goes dead.

Tomorrow, I'm catching a plane to Moscow. My flight is booked, a car is booked. Yesterday I picked up my visa from the issuing office in Clerkenwell. Lyuba took off with the children to see her parents a couple of weeks ago. Our dog is staying with friends. Summer has been neatly parceled up and everything is falling into place. I feel like Tintin on his first adventure into the land of the Soviets: ahead of me lies vodka, caviar, and intrigue, a theatre set primed with fake news and evil assassins, but unlike Tintin I want to put this all to one side, to un-see it, to keep it out of mind.

From my window is a view of trees, and through a gap in the trees the yellow of cornfields. A set of matrioshkas given to me last year are lined up on my desk. The painted wooden dolls show five Russian leaders, beginning with a large Putin and ending with a tiny, unopenable Lenin. In the middle are Stalin, Yelstin, and Medvedev. They are all armless, pudgy, inscrutable, done up in suits and ties and revolutionary tunics, and shining under layers of varnish.

Lyuba told me that a full set of leaders would be easy to find, yet it's hard to see how the toy makers could have made more and still kept them looking convincingly different. Already the five patriarchal dollies merge into each other, with their same-shaped bodies and heads. They all look across the table with the same enigmatic expression, and inside each is a story that leads back to the first doll, the tiny unopenable Lenin with a red ribbon painted onto his coat.

...

I was six when I first imagined Russia as a snowy exotica stuffed with troikas and fur hats. My family lived in south London, in a large falling-apart house under the shadow of the Crystal Palace television tower. I remember a lake with ducks and poplars, a neighbour's afternoon party where women danced in a slow sexual way, a kindly lodger called Freida, and a drunk who lived in the basement. I couldn't see much wrong with it, but in 1971 my father decided that pleasing my mother was high on his list of priorities, and he exchanged the crumbling red-brick mansion with its dodgy tenants and overgrown garden for a more modest house in Chorleywood, a small commuter town at the end of the Metropolitan line about forty minutes from Baker Street. There were rows of Edwardian villas, a few out-of-the-way pubs, and a rambling common where we exhausted ourselves playing football on tussocky grass. Beyond the train tracks you could see the council estate spreading over the hill. It was the sort of place where nothing ever happened. The station platform was always busy in the morning and at the end of each afternoon a steady stream of not-so-tired-looking men walked the last part of their way home.

My father was part of this well-mannered crowd during the day, but in the evenings and on weekends he set himself apart, and spent his time campaigning against nuclear weapons. His old Remington had extra-long type bars that echoed the run of his thoughts as they whacked against the roller. Sometimes as part of this work he copied already-written letters in duplicate, with sheets of blue carbon between the double papers, and then the chatter of keys ran almost without pause, flying through the rooms like bullets.

My mother played the piano. There were concerts and practice, and during those first months after we moved the sound of Fauré's Impromptus and Debussy's *Jardins sous la pluie* and *L'isle Joyeuse* filled the house with an unworldly mood, but I don't recall the two sounds, the music and the typing, both together at the same time. The music still evokes certain particular memories: the smell of potted hyacinths, slow drifting summer clouds, the rich patina of our chess table with its wobbly leg. The typing belongs to a different place, somewhere darker, uncertain, and full of disquiet for what was to come.

Our only coming together as a family was at breakfast, which was taken rather formally in the new dining room with the wireless tuned into Radio Three. We had our own chairs, our own plates and cutlery. My brother had a spoon with *Albion Hotel* engraved onto the handle. My spoon was long-handled with a small scoop and was stamped *Fortes Ice Cream Parlour*. It took a while for the brown wireless to warm up. After it was switched on the internal bulb began to glow, bringing into focus the names of European cities etched into the glass front. Then the music emerged through a fuzz and crackle of static, as through a thick fog. My father liked to guess who the piece was by before it came to an end and would encourage me to join in. I thought between slurps of cereal: was it Palestrina or Scarlatti? Haydn or Mozart? French music was easy to recognise once you got the knack of it. English music too. Sibelius was instantly recognisable, though there were moments when he sounded just like Tchaikovsky. Rachmaninoff also sounded like Tchaikovsky.

My mother kept quiet during these exchanges, as did Martin, my brother. It was a game between my father and myself. Martin was four years older than me, and wanted to be a guitarist in a rock group. He dreamed of escape, but he was a long way from that goal and we still looked out for each other. We understood that members of one family living under the same roof might have different ideas and yet share the same restrictions. Martin was not so interested in classical music and I was too young to rebel. It wasn't such a big deal. Life was still easy, and while our father deliberated in his uncommitted way between this or that composer, we both took the opportunity to spread as much peanut butter as we could onto our toast, hoping this wouldn't be noticed in the general excitement as the final chords struck home and the presenter's unhurried voice came on air.

It was in this house in Chorleywood, around the time of my tenth birthday, that I came into possession of a giant but incomplete U.S. military map of the Soviet Union. I'm not sure where it came from. It's possible that I picked it up from Stamfords on one of my trips to London. Or it could have been a gift from a colleague of my father's at the polytechnic in Walthamstow where he taught, one of those who knew of my hobby-like interest in things Russian. In any case it was unusual, made up as it was of three huge sheets that fitted together unevenly in a staggered pattern, the edges slanting off at oblique angles. I remember laying the map out on the floor of my bedroom so that I could fold the overlaps more accurately. Then I cleared the wall of my old posters and stuck it in place using the black lines of the railways to join the sheets as best as I could. Once it was up the massive shape took over the whole wall, beginning at the ceiling and finishing out of sight, below the line of my old striped mattress. To the east of Moscow, Russia extended as far as the Ural mountains. The Caspian Sea showed like the tip of somebody's tongue poking up at the bottom, while Arkhangelsk hovered in the frozen north, a dark smudge below the heavy hump of the Kola Peninsula.

It was a time of power-reckoning in the world. Nuclear military complexes ranged across the northern hemisphere, each load aimed at the other with a promise of mutually assured destruction. Nixon was in Moscow, and Brezhnev welcomed him at the Kremlin with much pomp and ceremony. There was a state banquet, and in the following days Nixon made a speech that was broadcast on television and radio. He was filmed sitting behind an ornate gilt desk with his back to a wall, talking of peace and cooperation, of joint ventures in space, of an end to misery, disease, and hunger in the world. It was a speech crafted in words and phrases carefully chosen to skirt around the very edge of a problem that was still gathering and growing. Fear was open and raw, the problem swung this way and that, unwieldy and repulsive, and yet Russia and America had chosen to talk, to smile, and to pose with pens and non-proliferation agreements. *Time* magazine splashed an image on its front cover of Brezhnev and Nixon caught in a light-hearted moment. Nixon looked on as Brezhnev delivered what seemed to be the punchline to a good joke. Nobody would ever get to know what it was he actually said, but their mutual smiles marked the beginning of a movement towards a resolution of something unimaginably bad, and this awakening of a new form of responsibility immediately began to spread, filtering slowly downwards through the various layers of society until, in the end, everybody was affected. The problem that had settled in without asking wouldn't go away, and there was nothing to be done. It was like living near a huge pile of rotting manure: you couldn't escape the smell even if you wanted to.

My recollections of this time divide into two distinct kinds. The first are clear, focused and unambiguous, while the second are always attached to particular events or people, and clouded in uncertainty. In the first kind of memory I see Chorleywood as if no time had passed, as if it were right here and now, unchanged and still living and breathing. I remember wide pavements and smooth speckled driveways, the smell of creosoted fences, clipped lawns, the plangent formality of cypress trees, magnolias in full bloom, happy-style families, fathers with jobs in town, mothers with degrees and interests, households trying to outdo each other with their ornaments and their holidays in France. In this first version there was no steadier or safer place to live, nowhere less corrupted by normal everyday suffering. But in the second version, the version that was connected to events and to people, a huge sadness hung over everything.

I was too young to understand this sadness but I could feel it. I knew that other people suffered, and that their world was also composed of two halves, the outside half where everything was clear and obvious, and an inside half, tangled with difficulties. My 'inside half' was the impressionable part of me. When I was home from school, most of my time was spent in the bedroom where the triple-sheet map formed a permanent backdrop to my thoughts and dreams. Sometimes I replaced the yellowed sellotape when it stopped sticking to the wall. Over one summer the staggered sheets faded to three different shades of green. Moscow radiated purple strands eastwards, the centre of a web that would have stretched, in a more complete map, over the whole of the Soviet Union. I repeated the odd-sounding names under my breath like magic charms - Pskov, Ufa, Smolensk, Kazan. Smoke stacks and other 'vertical obstructions' were marked with black dashes. There were light blue lakes and repeated dark green pine-tree motifs representing taiga. Information which had at first seemed cryptic turned out to be simple and practical. Crosshatched areas showed peat cuttings. Landmark features included churches, factories, monuments and slag piles. Bogs were drawn with horizontal blue dashes. I was struck by the size of these bogs. There were bogs the size of Switzerland, lakes the size of Portugal. Over time the image of a face formed itself across the patchy green sheets until it became the perfect outline of an old bearded man, made up of varying shades of taiga and tundra and bog, and the purple spread of towns.

In those days I was often ill, and had waking nightmares when the map over my bed became a real place, a kind of prison from which two flawed and compromised personalities fought for my attention. One voice, slow and cynical, told me not to worry, that everything was okay and that I only needed to stay put. The other voice, over-excited, hysterical and garbled, urged me to get out before it was too late. And so it went on, one voice after the other, until I felt as if I was going to explode in frustration.

Only my grandmother seemed to have some idea of the map's influence over me. She lived in Wales and we didn't see her very often. She stayed with us at Easter, and twice a year we drove down to Cardiff in one or other of our old cars that was always inclined to break down. Her evangelical faith towered over us, my father especially, and we ran away from it as if from something mad. I was able to keep myself to myself when I was down there, and even managed to lie convincingly about my progress at school which was actually quite poor. She had wanted to be a missionary and now she tried to make me promise to give myself to God too, in some equally amazing way. She took my hands in a grip that was surprisingly firm and difficult to pull away from: 'Be a fine, upright man, Stephen,' she said, 'A gentleman!' Then, with her eyes closed and head tilted back, she invoked the Lord's divine intervention on behalf of a sinner.

Her bedroom was out of bounds but I remember once, when the house was empty, plucking up the courage to enter. I pushed open her door and was met by a smell of camphor, dark polished furniture, and heavy rose-patterned curtains. A large crucifixion picture hung over the dressing table showing Jesus nailed up between two strong-man thieves. I looked at it for a long time, fascinated by the expression of agony on Jesus's face and the odd blue colour of the blood that oozed from a slit in his side. On the way out I caught sight of myself in the wardrobe mirror. A pale adolescent face was reflected in the glass, and for the first time but not the last time in my life I saw something knowing and cruel, like death, staring back at me.

It was a relief to be back home where my soul was not expected to perform, and where I could keep all my other sordid secrets safely hidden - my collection of porn magazines and my Monty Python book with its jokes about masturbation and defecation. But I couldn't hide the map, and when my grandmother visited and came up to my room it became clear that this was the worst of my sins. She stood quietly, resolutely, her stick planted firmly in the carpet, one hand gripping the table as if steadying herself against the force of evil that seemed to be zoning in on her.

'A godless empire!' she said at last, as if invoking her final judgement on my character, and that I was, to all intents and purposes, lost forever to the workings of the devil.

•••

A life can be divided up into places. I can divide up mine between houses that have come and gone: our first family house in south London, then the house in Chorleywood, later there was another move further into the countryside, and then London again for all my work years. Now I am in Suffolk. In one way or another Russia runs like a thread through all of these places. Sometimes its intrusion can be explained logically, the result of particular circumstances. But its influence has also been arbitrary and unlooked for, like a fluke result which keeps repeating itself.

The film *Little Vera* went on general release in England in 1988. I saw it in the Odeon on the Kings Road with a friend of mine, Richard Patterson. We had both finished art college and were unemployed and without funds to help us get by. Richard had arranged for me to help him re-lay a patio in a house not far from the cinema. The patio-laying paid well and afterwards we had enough money to go for a drink and then to the cinema without worrying about the cost. *Little Vera* was the first Soviet film to include a sex scene but it began quite differently, with a long slow shot of apartment blocks and factory chimneys. I had never seen anything so incredible, neither in real life nor in films. The scale of life as depicted in this opening, even as the credits still rolled down the screen, had a great effect on me. The rows of identical windows and balconies, the monstrous tubes and steel supporting structures, the lines of red-barred brick chimneys spewing plumes of white smoke that rose and then drifted off to one side, acted like a slow-working drug on my system. It was as if the unconscious and the conscious had fused together in a waking state, where past and present and future were all rolled into one.

It's difficult to know where to begin. Sometimes I think it all started with the map, but it could equally have begun in that small cinema with the red plush seats where I watched *Little Vera*, or on that rainy evening when I was taken to a party in Shepherd's

Bush where I first met Lyuba. A year later we visited a barbed wire enclosure with portakabin offices in Sheerness, with a rehearsed story designed to convince the authorities of the worthiness of our marital intentions. To start on that grey day on that barren strip of land on the Thames estuary has a symmetry, as it later turned out, but the logical story begins when I first took a train to Russia.

The Paris-Moscow train left Gare de l'Est in the evening. It was the spring of 1989, a year that was to turn into one of the most momentous for Europe since the end of the war. Protests took on a growing energy that turned out to be unstoppable. Huge crowds gathered in city squares in Romania, Bulgaria, Poland, Czechoslovakia, Hungary, and East Germany. They were met by riot police with shields and truncheons, but the real power of the communist regimes had already seeped away. Ceausescu and his wife were dragged onto a street in Bucharest and shot. On the ninth of November an executive order came from the ruling East Germany party allowing freedom of movement westwards. The first holes in the Berlin Wall were smashed through. On the streets everywhere people popped champagne corks and embraced strangers. The forces of organised repression were in full retreat, all those small acts of rebellion which had been unthinkable suddenly became possible; people felt free and they expressed this freedom with innocent smiles. Border guards standing awkwardly with their weapons shook hands with civilians who looked hesitant and uncertain, as if they couldn't believe what was happening. All kinds of informers melted into the shadows. In Dresden, an undercover agent called Adamov, whose real name was Vladimir Vladimirovich Putin, spent what were to be his last days in Germany in the basement of a house on Angelika Strasse destroying memos in a furnace, frantically keeping the flames going with a poker, pondering his next move while a crowd gathered on the street outside.

After my train passed Minsk I found myself sharing the compartment with a man from Burkina Faso, one of the last of the scholarship students invited to study by the Soviet government as part of a cold war charm offensive in Africa. John Updike talks of a Russian delegation descending on Rabat in 1969, of a dark-suited column of bureaucrats arriving in Morocco with a deal and no sham English smiles. Afterwards the Russians were given a three-day tour that began at the docks in Casablanca, where the governor talked of the extraordinary rapport that existed between the two countries on all levels. King Hassan did not commit to their offer in the end, but elsewhere across Africa the Soviets made steady progress.

While the pine forests of Eastern Europe opened up to either side of the track, my travelling companion reached under his seat for a small suitcase. He put it on the folding table in front of him and unzipped the soft top with an air of inscrutability. It turned out to be full of ladies' underwear of all different sorts, panties and suspenders and corsets and bras. All kinds of lingerie in black and scarlet colours, cheap-looking stuff with lace and ribbons jumbled together in an untidy knot. He told me in English that he was going to sell it and that this would cover his expenses. Expenses for what? I asked. He didn't reply. For a long time he sorted through it, fingering it and untangling it, holding it up, scrutinising it. I wondered about the money, and of who would be putting on these tiny slips of material, and of what passions they would ignite.

Lyuba met me off the train. It was the end of March and the snow was all gone. The long platform was almost empty and everything was dusty in the spring sunshine. We stayed all over the place, sometimes at her flat on Presnensky Val, sometimes at her parents' flat to the south of the city opposite the Lefortovo jail where Solzhenitsyn was charged with treason and deprived of his Soviet citizenship. Sometimes we stayed in friends' apartments, communal apartments with tall-ceilinged rooms that had been portioned up from grand houses of the Moscow aristocracy. They were always grubby and overrun with cockroaches that hid in the cracks behind heating pipes, and under cookers in the filthy kitchens. Huge windows, thick with dirt, gave light onto balustraded staircases, and in the corners and unused spaces a special kind of drabness gathered, an accumulation of dust and grease, and a heavy sense of endings.

We took the overnight train south, to Crimea. The Soviet establishment decamped there every summer and we had no thought of doing something different. From Simferopol, we took a taxi to the small resort town of Sudak, famous for its castle and its rock. What can I remember about that time? Strawberries, a sagging bed, hot sand, Lyuba covered in pieces of paper from head to foot as a ruse to prevent sunburn, an inedible hunk of yellowish salt fish, a quayside of the south with its hot southern smells, a rusty trawler flying the most romantic flag in the world – entirely red with a yellow hammer and sickle in the top corner. I remember a walnut tree and a line of single storey holiday lets. The last room next to the outside kitchen had a stable door that was always kept shut, and was home to a pig. You would hear its snuffles and snorts, and occasionally a full-blown squeal. Perhaps it was hungry. We lay and listened on our sagging bed, still burning with energy from the sun and sea, as happy as two people might be who couldn't quite fuse their bodies into one.

In the morning we turned and greeted each other without irony, after the sleep which had kept us apart. By midday the sun had heated the tin-roofed room to such a degree of stuffiness that we were forced out into the glare. Big steel pots hung in the coolness of the washroom. We heated water to make tea in turns, with an electric element dangled in the cup. Then we took the road which led to the sea. I was interested in Lyuba's family and her life. There was nothing I liked more than to listen to her stories of Moscow intrigues, of her crazy aunts and uncles, and of their connections. For the first time I had found someone who understood motives, who could describe a person's life through obsession, or lust, or weakness, or through the various sacrifices they might have made. I had never thought of these things in such a clear way before.

We returned when our money ran out and spent the rest of the summer in Bolshevo, a quiet suburb half an hour from Moscow, on the way to the old monastic town of Zagorsk. I read and cycled and attended karate lessons. I swam in the river and got to know Boris, Lyuba's four-year-old son. In Moscow I was taken around the sites by Lyuba's uncle, Leonid, who had an encyclopedic memory for classic texts, and a stylish dress sense of the type you used to see in the old Martini adverts. We visited Red Square on a damp September evening. Beyond the granite mausoleum the red-brick walls of the Kremlin towered over the line of Norway spruces. I explained in my halting Russian that the double pointed turrets running along the top reminded me of a town in Italy.

'Which town?' Leonid asked.

I told him that it was Ferrara, and he recited some lines from Mandelstam's poem, *Ariosto*. Two years later he lost all the money he ever made and much more besides in a banking scam that swept unregulated Russia. He sold his flat to pay friends who had invested in him, then spent six more years working off his other debts before leaving Russia for good to begin a new life, studying the Torah and devoting himself to the demanding rituals and rules of Jewish orthodoxy in the small eastern German town of Chemnitz.

It makes sense to start from that first trip to Moscow, but that would mean it was a done story, and it isn't done. The Soviet Union was still alive when we stood on the salty quayside in Sudak under that slow-moving red flag. In those moments it didn't seem as if anything would end, and certainly not something as eternal-seeming as the integrity of the USSR. A long-restrained sensuality had broken open in both of us. It was like finding you can fly in a dream, and wanting to communicate how natural and easy it all is. I wrote to friends telling them of what had happened, of where I was, and of how lucky I felt myself to be.

Now every month brings news from Russia that sounds decisive and difficult. Old slogans are losing ground but old attitudes stay the same. It's as if the idea of Russia has been dislocated out of its socket, and everywhere there is an effort to put things back, to pin the country and its past down and explain it. I've gone over the many different events which are talked of as part of the record, and those from my own life, until they all join together like the stories of somebody who has too much to tell, and tells it too quickly, so that half the sense is missing. It's a tale of confusion, of compromise and love, and out of it, or rather always there in the background are the fanatical stories of new-Russia that keep coming, like a Baron Munchausen epic for the modern times.

My grandmother is long dead. She died while visiting my aunt in Coulsdon when I was twelve. It was snowing and we were taken to see her for the last time in an old Land Rover. Our car had broken and we'd borrowed a farm vehicle with a canvas top that flapped and a loose tailgate that rattled all the way to London. There was a vigil. We took it in turns beside the body. My cousins left and it was my family's turn, in the end it was just my turn. I found myself alone in the box room where she lay, no longer able to threaten me with divine retribution, or boredom. I sat and stared at her waxy face as if I could learn something from it, bending closer and looking for the last time at her domineering features, at her strong hands and the soft down that grew almost imperceptibly across her cheek and on her chin.

...

The room is dim. Over there by the table are my things, my bag and on the table next to the bag, my wallet and passport and printed ticket. Car keys. I didn't mean to fall asleep, and now I can't clear my head. What happened? I was on the sofa, propped with pillows, remembering. Such a pleasure to do that. I am like the old lady that Simone de Beauvoir wrote about, who spent ecstatic hours going over the simplest of childhood memories just before she died.

I can't decide what book to bring with me. On the table is a pile, all with a Russian theme. Russian writers on Russia, English writers on Russia. Polish writers on Russia. American writers on Russia. Then there are Russian writers on England, Russian writers on America, Ukrainian writers on Russia, Polish writers on Ukraine. A whole stack of books. There are novels and journalistic histories. A lot of working over the evils of Stalinism and Leninism. Books uncovering corruption. Political analyses of the oligarchs, sensational books about the oligarchs. Books on the gulag. Lots of piggybacking on the suffering of innocents. Statistics of death, listed and mulled over. Statistics of injustice, mulled over, declaimed.

On top of one of the piles is a book on Benjamin Britten left here last week by Lena, a friend from London. She is one of those we came into contact with through mutual Russian acquaintance.

She has two young children that she brings up on her own, lives in a flat in Sydenham, gives music lessons, organises events in the Russian community, and has a family history that straddles borders and eras. Her Siberian-born grandparents escaped eastwards from the Bolsheviks to the Russian sector of Shanghai in 1920, and were amongst those caught up in the many stories of compromised returns and flights abroad again. Half her family live in Vancouver, but her mother lives in Yekaterinburg. Now Lena wants to move to Tunbridge Wells.

In London, there is still a whole crowd of these friends: Lena, Anna, Anya, Tanya, Marina, Olya. There is something direct about them that cuts nicely through the muddled English shyness. Partners come and go, and there is often trouble. We used to have a tree in the front garden, a mimosa, that Lyuba planted some years ago to remind her of home. Mimosas grow fast and it wasn't long before it towered over the privet hedge. Every spring it produced a great froth of bright yellow flowers. This was the blossom that was passed around in Moscow on International Women's Day. The mimosa sprigs were brought up from the southern republics where it was already warm in the beginning of March. The blossoms reminded Lyuba of her schooldays, and after a few years of living in England she began handing them out to our Russian women friends, to Lena, Anna, Anya, Tanya, Marina, and Olya, in damp, chilly London.

When Lena visited last week she brought her old teacher from the conservatoire in St Petersburg. Her teacher had spent the previous night at Benjamin Britten's house in Aldeburgh. She was an academic, pale and unhealthy looking, with a tunnel-like thinking taken from books; a scholar with a scholar's way of interpreting everything through the prism of learning.

We walked down the weedy path towards the overgrown orchard where a powerline runs overhead. It was getting late and the light was fading. We stopped for a while under the old yew next to the potting shed wall. Apples showed. They were already red but we could hardly see the colour in the dimmness. They looked simply grey.

'How are you going to make your garden? In the English style or the French?' she asked me with a wry smile.

I looked at the overgrown brambles running along the bottom hedge. Lena was playing with her two boys in front of the house. Screams of excitement floated across the lawn, then the sound of a ball being booted. After that, more screams and frantic orders from a deeper, resentful voice. It was Grigory, the elder boy, who always found himself having to give in to his younger brother. Sometimes it reduced him to tears, this terrible fraternal injustice.

'Maybe in the English style?' I suggested.

Lena's old teacher seemed satisfied.

'I prefer it,' she said.

Lena looked over and waved. I waved back and then turned to her old teacher who had begun talking all about England, about Tunbridge Wells, about Benjamin Britten, and about Aldeburgh. It was a great relief when I dropped them at the station the following morning.

Everything has begun cracking up - at least that's what it seems like to me. From a distance Russia resembles a large chunk of ice floating in a drink, becoming ever more transparent, slowly melting at the edges. Before you know it, another bit has fallen off. The thought of how things seem in Russia, and of how things really are, keeps everyone guessing. Sometimes I recognise what used to be called 'the spirit of the place' when I watch old Russian movies. It hasn't been put there by the director or written into the script, but it's there all the same. It's in old news coverage of the May Day parades, in the voices of presenters that always dripped with tolerant humanity. It's in the details, in the morning preparations caught on camera, in the leaves that move even when the weather looks settled, in the sense of occasion. It fills the spaces around the real-time events, and has been preserved, as if forever, on videotape. It's in the voices that describe a world that will never change, though it doesn't correspond exactly to the sense of what is said, any more than it does now, when the same people talk of nostalgia for the beautiful past, or of how Russia might be created all over again, as if from scratch.

3

There are twenty minutes to landing. The seat belt lights are on and we are descending through lines of massed white clouds to Domodedovo airport. Shadows stream upwards through the cabin, from the cockpit to the galley. My book, testaments of Chernobyl survivors, remains unopened in the magazine pouch in front of me.

A map of Russia is sketched in my notebook. It has the shape of a piece of liver, or a mythological animal with two heads and a clumsy, pot-bellied body. I have marked Moscow, and Lyuba's village of Vashutino, and a line which connects them both and then runs southwards in a Russian Г shape to a blob at the bottom that is supposed to be Crimea. It's the route map of a holiday we have yet to take as a family, a lazy holiday to spend on the beach, and afterwards in the Grand Astoriya Hotel in Feodosia, or one of the shack-like holiday lets that rent out in summer all along the coast.

In the margin of the map I have scribbled the outline of a story that begins when Russia was still pinned to my bedroom wall, and continues through the pangs of adolescence to the discovery of freedom and love. Beyond this is a blur, a long period of life that seems missing, as if it didn't quite add up. Whole decades have passed in which I have no lasting recollections, not without working through things that happened on particular events or dates. It's as if I've been dumped here straight from an earlier time, like those people who come out after a long stretch in prison and have to pick up where they left off and start living all over again.

I pick out an old photo stored on my phone, a black and white snapshot with a thin white border that shows me on my father's shoulders. He looks happy, almost carefree, and not how I remember him. I look serious, worried, as if the weight of the world was already pressing down on me. The light sets into relief a frown in the middle of my forehead, a crease of concerned concentration that looks as if it would never go away.

Through the window a curve of new buildings stands out in the strong sun. There are reservoir tanks covered in duck weed, clusters of dachas, a motorway. Trees whizz past, then some low buildings and a group of planes parked up.

At the customs a young guard stops me and asks me where I'm going and what I'm planning on doing. 'I'm going to see my family,' I say. Then he asks how much cash I'm bringing into the country, and I tell him that my wallet is empty. He laughs and lets me through.

Everything is easier than it was, smoother, more relaxed. Gone is the military-styled interrogation and the sense that you are passing into a place from which a safe return is not certain. Now it could be any airport, anywhere in the world, except for the lingering smell, a mixture of sweetness and putridity just like the special smell of the Moscow underground, only not so strong.

Outside it's warm. Taxi drivers are playing backgammon in the corner of the parking lot, balancing their board between the openings of a metal ventilation grill. I'm given a late model Chrysler with an asymmetrical dashboard and a wonderful new-car smell, and invited to enjoy it. Before starting the engine I send a message to Lyuba, a line of union jacks and an emoji face wearing dark glasses. She replies with a line of question marks. So I send her a Russian flag instead, and that seems to do the trick. She replies with 'Better...'

I speed a little too fast out of the airport, flipping through the radio stations and keeping an eye on the big overhead signs. For a while I listen to a telephone call-in show. The host's voice exudes oily authority:

'Pokemon – the question for those of you who've just joined us: are we safe? '

The have-a-go callers are discussing the first Pokemon-inspired murder in Guatemala. The word Pokemon rises strangely out of the heavy flow of Russian. The presenter dwells on the word, repeating it many times over in his deeply male voice until it begins to sound as if he is completely off his head. I switch to a station playing Wagner. The orchestra brings Tannhauser to a thundering climax, while heroically-sized billboards rise up on either side of the road advertising real estate, mega shopping complexes, election candidates.

The route into town is traffic free. I was warned of the terrible congestion, and only yesterday I read that the old beautiful Moscow is being smashed up and replaced with something disgusting and new, yet the empty streets are mellow and looked-after. It seems to me as if it couldn't be better, as if you couldn't do a better job. Tables are out on the pavements beneath awnings. People are going about their business. Suddenly and unexpectedly, I see the twisted lolly-swirls of St Basil's Cathedral. It's surprisingly close, just beyond the buildings at the end of the road, and for a moment out of all this poised elegance comes something different, like noticing a rip for the first time in the fabric of a beautiful tapestry, or feeling a cold draught when you know that all the doors are shut. The image looks grey, tired, old. On the other side of the square, the towers and domes of the Kremlin with their crooked gold crosses are more numerous than I remember, like a rash of antennae, waiting, listening, calculating.

I drive along the embankment keeping my eye on the red-brick walls and towers, and the cluster of golden domes, for as long as possible. They seem to me like the nerve centre of a creature that cannot quite control itself, that has no choice but to listen and calculate endlessly. When I first walked around them Gorbachev was dreaming of a progressive socialism. He was one of the younger men of the generation who had supported Krushchev's reforms and then kept quiet through Brezhnev's era of corrupt stagnation. A year after he became General Secretary, the nuclear reactor at Chernobyl blew up. The attempt to cover up the extent of the disaster was even more damaging to his image than the poorly installed systems which had triggered the biggest nuclear accident in history, and little by little the press was given more slack. Glasnost, the concept of slightly more openness in public life, was invented to combat the heavy weight of cynicism that had been suffocating the spirit of Socialism for so long. A policy of change was introduced - Perestroika - but nobody was quite satisfied. The proposals were either too incredible or not incredible enough, depending on who you asked. A great responsibility had descended on the shoulders of politicians, and they responded by rolling up their shirt sleeves and squaring their shoulders. Now is the time! they said. Then they retreated again. The facade of stability and togetherness that had kept the Brezhnev era alive was crumbling away, and it turned out there was nothing solid to replace it with.

I used to cycle around Moscow to keep fit. Russia was a great playground, an amazing and exciting land that I had been given the key to, quite by chance. Close up to the walls, round the back of the Kremlin, and not far from the site of the old Moscow open-air pool that used to steam all winter like an Icelandic geyser, I was knocked to the side, literally carried off my feet by a sonic wave, a super-loud piercing boom fired from the first of the black cars in the presidential motorcade exiting through the rear gates.

It seemed Gorbachev was great; everybody in England thought so. Here was a Soviet leader who didn't cast an evil eye over the world, who didn't appear paranoid or greedy, who wasn't anxious to puff himself up, or to knock somebody down, who seemed kind, tolerant, open. Everything was simple. For the first time in my life I was completely happy. What did I care about wars, about power, or intrigue? It didn't bother me if I managed to do something worthwhile or not. Everything was still before me, and there was no rush to get things done.

Now it isn't so easy to dodge the forces of opinion. In London I watch pro-Kremlin news on the computer and find myself talking to people who support Russia without question, and to those who claim to have been betrayed by Russia's leaders. I attend Russian-themed talks by well meaning English academics, and listen to the harangues of cynical Russian hacks. I read of dollar bills piling up in empty apartments, of billions of euros moving through offshore accounts, of sex trades, of losers, alcoholics and dullards, of mysticism and holiness, of bodily renunciation, self-castigation, auto-castration, fasting, fanatical purity, assassinations, arbitrary arrests, endless playground-bullying, misinformation, criminal-style falsifications. I read of the gullible who are controlled by television, and of the helpless who watch in disbelief as their country sinks further into a pit of badness. Whenever there is talk of Russia these themes turn up. Too much happens in too short a time, and nothing connects to the real event. Everything feeds back to one oligarch, one corrupt general, one fanatical monk. It's as if the information has all been written by the same hand, conceived by the same inspiritation. Energy runs vertically through life, and floating on the mixture is the one ruler, the big sticky cherry, untouchable on the top.

I buy cornflowers from a couple working the queue of cars building up on Prospekt Mira. The man passes a bunch through my open window and asks for what seems to me a massive sum. I've forgotten the exchange rate and the bills in my wallet don't yet mean anything to me. His tanned arm reaches in for the money. I can see the dirt under his broken fingernails and the rough skin of his open palm. Cars are hooting, a big space has opened up in front of us. I give him a bill, then another one, then I root around in my pocket for some change. He wants more but I say it's too much and move forward to join the queue that's inching forward under the famous statue *Worker and Kolkhoz Woman*, both of them reaching high into the air with their sacred tools of labour.

He's gone and I have a little moment of regret. Lyuba would say that if you spend money it goes away - that your money, such as it is, becomes less, and that this is something you should keep in mind. And yet neither is she particularly careful. The traffic is still slow and the flower vendor isn't far away. There's nothing to stop me calling out to him. To give him an extra note would make no difference to me, but already it feels too late, as if I had missed a chance. I watch him in my mirror for a while, talking to his partner next to the crash barriers by the side of the road, until he disappears behind the curve of cars.

We crawl forward, inching our way out of town. There is something soft about the political advertisements. Huge faces dominate each junction. Flawlessly aged men stare across the long lines of cars with expressions of such intense openness that they resemble babies. Each time I come here the style of the place is different, sometimes a lot different. In London, the view of Russia changes too, but more slowly. In our house a miniature version of events always used to run its cycle, a little Russia was nurtured, thrived, grew, died away, popped up amongst the Englishness, and was supplanted again.

Lyuba wanted the children to speak Russian well. More than that, she wanted to speak to them in Russian, to be Russian with them. For them and her to interract Russianly, for *them* to be Russian. They were already English, but they were not yet quite Russian. If you spoke Russian, if you formed your thoughts using Russian, did that mean that you thought differently? Certainly something was different. The thoughts came out with a slightly different flavour, the same thoughts but a different style. And the pitch of the voice was different too, the words changed the way the throat worked so that the sounds came out deeper and fruitier.

How can you plan for what lies ahead? One way is to place a scrunched up paper on a tray, burn it, then look into the ashes and read the future. A woman from Oryol told me this trick, and I believed her enough to provide a tray for the experiment, a lacquered tin tray decorated with a picture of a sabre-wielding Cossack, a wedding present from Lyuba's mother. After the ashes had been read there was a dirty mark on the tray where the picture had burnt through. I tried washing it and scrubbing with a rag, but couldn't get rid of a dark smudge that took away the Cossack's face and part of the landscape in the background.

Now I work through my problems in the same way that the lady from Oryol used to look into the future. I tell myself things like: 'This summer holiday seems to be following the pattern of our separated lives in England.' Or: 'Lyuba took a plane last week. I guess that means she's left without me...' Or: 'I don't care what you say, if two people live in different places, they're living apart!'

I tell myself these things and then they become things that have happened. Maybe it's different for the children. They slip between their different lives easily. Lyuba is more like me, and soon begins to give up her English habits when it comes to what she calls 'going home'. The thought of Russia, of her young life spent here, and of the whole scope of things which have moved on or disappeared (in her life, and in Russia), is enough to make her see things as they once were again. It hardly matters what she wants to do in Russia. It hardly matters, even, *who* is there.

Her enthusiasm always takes me by surprise because our life in London had never been an emigrant's life. It had never felt foreign in that way. The party where we met had been a Burns Night bash hosted by a friend of a friend, a writer called Jim Campbell who worked for the T.L.S. The flat was cramped and busy, with the usual huge pile of coats in the bedroom, the small kitchen where haggis was served, and the front room with the sofa and the bookshelves and the standing lamps. Lyuba arrived with a man called Zinik, and his wife, Nina. Lyuba was visiting England for the first time and staying with them in Lewisham. Zinik was a writer, and a cousin of Lyuba's mother, and had lived in London since the 1970's. I remember his well tailored blue-striped shirt, the twist in his back which became more pronounced over the years, and the one-sided look of concentration as he talked in the crowded room. His novels and short stories were all about emigration in its various forms. Sometimes this emigration (which in his case was an emigration with no promise of return) became a sort of exile in his writing. He talked of forgetting his keys, of walking out of his front door, closing it behind him and then, unable to get back into his flat, of being shut out as if a barrier had come down between himself and the rest of the world, a barrier as hermetically efficient as those sliding doors that swished shut in the Star Trek shows he liked to watch on television. He had photos of himself taken at the passport office after being sworn in as a British Citizen, turning in the booth as if he had been surprised by the flash. He wrote of himself and of his family, of his father who lost a leg in the war fighting on the Russian side, and of his grandfather who had studied in Berlin. The idea of emigration, exile, loss, and a sense of Jewish estrangement from the establishment, was wrapped up in all sorts of different forms and presented as the main idea and driver behind his books, and even his actual identity as a person.

This life felt a million miles away from Lyuba's and mine. To worry about our position in this way never occurred to us. At a certain moment we realised that we needed to live together, and in the end we chose England. For a hundred reasons it was easier to begin in England, and so it happened. At least this is how I always thought. But now I'm not so sure of my version of events. It's become harder to talk of 'us', because 'us' is no longer an accurate expression. The 'us' position takes too much for granted, and my surprise at Lyuba's enthusiasm for leaving England to 'go home' shows up the mistake.

Beyond Rizhsky Puteprovod the traffic starts to flow again, and for a short while out of Moscow the Arkhangelsk road becomes a grand five-lane motorway. It takes just under two hours to reach Pereslavl, and then the road returns to how it used to be, a single carriageway with a gritty hard shoulder. Dark woods close in on either side. Sometimes there are gaps in the trees. A way off leads to a shallow clearing with stumps and a pile of blackening logs. A huge field stretches into the distance. Then there are more woods. Pine woods. Oak woods. All sorts of scrappy woods. Trees that have fallen over. Trees that have fallen but remain propped up against their still-living neighbours. Wild hops and bindweed crawl everywhere over this confusion. Creepers of all kinds spread on the ground, across bushes, up telegraph poles. Everything is smothered with growth, as if it had been coated in a layer of green goo.

I pass a tank sitting on a rock-like plinth, its gun turret aimed high over the streaming traffic into the pines. This tank memorial is the landmark to look out for. Opposite is a roadside cafe with a cindered parking lot, big enough for lorries to pull up and take a rest, and a little further on is another smaller cafe where there is a sign for Tereskal.

For the first half mile the road is covered in potholes, deep crevices, and rifts. It has become worse over the years, and I go slowly from side to side, trying not to put a hole in the bottom of the rental car. The road climbs and falls, and then climbs again until the woods open up and a lake comes into view. For a short while the church of Romanovo appears in the distance, then the land falls away and the lake and the church disappear in the trees.

The first wooden houses are set back on their own, behind tall fences. It's not much of a place. There's no shop or village hall. Our house is by a pond though you cannot see this from the road. I park up in the weeds by the high slatted fence. There's nobody in the garden. The front door is open and the heavy leather-covered inner door gives with a good shove. Children's stuff lies everywhere. Daisy's bag is opened on the kitchen floor. Miles's baseball cap with Dodgers printed across the front is on top of the cooker.

Everything looks just as it was. The Russian stove, the pechka, still takes up most of the space in what is now a bedroom. Probably it would still be used if the house was lived in over winter, but it remains unlit, year on year, and smells of dust and damp. I walk past the piano and into a larger room where another stove has recently been installed, a new one made in Spain with a glass door. This one is lit in rainy weather when it would otherwise be too dreary to sit in the shadows doing nothing. The cracks between the logs of the walls are stuffed with wool. Here it smells of the new pine panelling in the spare room, and the deal table that's used as a worktop for the sewing machine. Beyond the spare room is an annex with a kitchen.

Lyuba bought the house and the small plot of land it stands on with money from the sale of the old family dacha that was close to Moscow. The old shared place was demolished to make way for blocks of flats during the first wave of property speculation that swept through Russia in the 90's. Since then new developments have sprung up every year within driving distance of Moscow. They are all stamped with the same Bavarian kitsch, and surrounded by the same metal fences. Vashutino was supposed to be far enough away to be free of this urbanisation, and yet even here new houses are going up. You can't see them from the village, but if you walk down the path towards the lake there is the beginning of what will become a tall metal enclosure. Earthworks have begun and everybody is talking about it. The new houses will have a view across to Romanovo, and issues have been raised about their legality, and whether the developers are building over a right of way that passes through the fields to one of the old swimming places.

It's quiet. The garden looks overgrown, the vegetable patches are empty. Where there used to be potatoes there is grass. Apple trees are loaded with fruit. There are some asters and nasturtiums and a strongly suckering dog rose. The pond is bigger than I remember and reeds grow thickly in the shallow water around the edge. The willow trees are shedding their leaves onto the muddy bank, even though they are still green. One of the old landing stages has gone, and half of the low fence that separates the garden from the bank is down, lying flat on the ground.

I pick out an open carton of kefir from the fridge and take a long drink. Then I go back outside and wait on the porch steps for somebody to turn up.

4

Daisy is shocked to see me. She's thirteen, skinny, tall. Her blonde hair has been trimmed at the front in a fringe. Her brown eyes are opened wide in surprise. For the moment she can't say anything. It's as if she's seen a ghost, or dreaming. I have to walk over and put my arm around her shoulder to unfreeze her.

'It's me!' I say.

At last she smiles. Miles, who is two years younger, looks pleased though it could be that he's only quicker at adjusting. Lyuba's mother, Olga, raises her hands in welcome as if she was surprised too, though she probably knew I was coming. Lyuba smiles at my predicament. Nikolai, Lyuba's father, is shocked, like Daisy.

I hand over the flowers. Last year I framed a photograph of Olga and Lyuba, taken when Lyuba was a young girl. I found the transparency in a plastic bag full of slides in a drawer in Suffolk and had it processed. The framed photo hangs on the wall, a gift to make up for an argument between the two of us. Well, that's over now, and all is back to how it was. This time it's just a simple birthday offering. Olga cuts the string and arranges the flowers in a vase. I sit on the sofa under the window and say a few things. The children reply to my questions reluctantly.

'We weren't expecting you,' Lyuba begins and then stops.

Nikolai clears a bag from one of the chairs at the table.

'Please!' he says, gesturing for me to sit down.

'You said you would cook pelmeni!' Miles is looking at his grandmother with wide-open, resentful eyes.

'Papa has arrived,' Olga replies pointedly.

I can already detect the old subtle ways, the games of manipulation that used to drive me to despair when we came together as a family. The children certainly didn't expect me, nor are they overjoyed at my presence. I used to visit more often, but for the past few years I've let it slip. There was always a good reason to stay in London, to keep working while the family was away, and now a Vashutino-routine has settled in a groove that doesn't include me, that thrives on my absence.

To see the family seemed like a good idea in England, but since they have been living without me the kids have begun to do things differently, to make jokes I don't share, to discover new ways of seeing things, even of eating differently. My turning up is an awkward reminder of something missing. Without realising, I have become the visitor whose presence makes everyone feel stilted, a father who expects either too much or nothing at all.

Olga puts some tvorog onto a dish, spoons honey over it and puts it on the oil cloth in front of Miles.

'Kushai! Kushai!' she says, and then asks Daisy if she wants some.

'Nu Baba, chto eto? Nu smotri!'

Olga has a piece of goose grass stuck to the back of her dress. Daisy picks it off, shows it, and puts it on the table between the dishes of salad and the glasses.

'Cho ty mne ne skazala?' Olga wants to know why she didn't tell her before, why Daisy allowed her grandmother to walk around all day with half of the garden hanging off her back. Daisy doesn't answer because she's spreading butter on a piece of bread, making it go all over while keeping the bread from tearing apart. Then she does the same with the caviar, coating the butter with a perfectly even layer of black cream. Miles is looking at the operation with the butter and the caviar with his mouth open, as if he was stuck in the middle of saying something.

Alya walks in. She's a neighbour from across the road and most likely knows I'm here, and has come to say hello. I get up and shake her hand. She wears a loose blue dress and her strandy grey hair is done up in a bun. Alya is an old college friend of Olga and has a daughter, Netka, who has similar aged children to our own. Netka has a husband who doesn't come to Vashutino. I've never seen him, though I've heard about him, and had descriptions from Lyuba.

He's a software engineer at a bank and finds Vashutino rough, at least that's what we hear, but perhaps he simply doesn't want to stay with Netka's family. As far as Alya is concerned, when Netka comes to Vashutino she is also having a holiday from her husband. And so there is a kind of symmetry to the neighbourly gatherings. Two mothers without husbands, two grandmothers rock steady behind them, two grandfathers trying to be manly and, under this umbrella of familial protection, various grandchildren and their friends. The party's all full up, and I don't fit in. And yet I'm here.

The children have left with their friends. I'm sitting on this bouncy sofa bed in the makeshift kitchen listening to Alya explain to Olga how she picks apples from the ground every day, and it feels as if I had slipped into a dream, or as if I'd walked through the map which was once sellotaped to my bedroom wall, and come out on the other side.

Nikolai brings in a bottle of brandy, the shock has passed and he's all smiles now. Alya gets up to leave, and Olga thanks her for the plate of cakes she has left. The cakes are on the table along with a beetroot salad and a plate of selyodka. Nikolai pours two glasses, a full one for me, and a bit in the bottom for himself. He's been ill, yet still looks enormously strong.

Olga puts hot boiled potatoes and a piece of chicken on my plate. We drink up, and I dab some butter on the potatoes and watch it melt. Then I fork a piece of selyodka, while Nikolai fills my glass again.

'To the children!' He proposes, his hand cradling the almost empty tumbler.

It's already quite late, around ten o'clock, and the children are over the road at Alya's. They are an easy subject for us. We are all fond of them, but it's still a relief that Olga is here, ready to fill any gap in the conversation. Awkward silences between Nikolai and myself are frequent. I used to fill the gap myself, but now I don't bother so much. There was a time when I thought that by letting the silence run its full course we might overcome the problem, which was not the actual silence but the awkwardness that lurked behind the silence. A disagreement lies somewhere at the bottom of our father-son-in-law contract, pushed ever further into the deep mud, hidden amongst those resentments that are always avoided for the sake of everybody's sanity and safety. It's as if he sees something new in me, something alien that must be dealt with. It poses an endless conundrum, and it seems there's nothing to remedy the situation. The awkwardness has gone on too long, and neither of us has the energy to do anything more about it.

Olga is looking at what Nikolai drinks, but she needn't worry. While he has been filling my glass he has hardly tasted his own. The children come in from outside looking tired and wildly untidy. Miles crashes on the divan bed next to the kitchen table and opens his iPad. Daisy goes to brush her teeth. Nikolai gets up and wishes me goodnight. Olga tells Miles to go and clean his teeth too.

'Baba!' he calls back, outraged.

Olga will stay up for a long time. That's always been her habit. The last one to bed, always pottering around the kitchen, usually with a phone in her hand. Cooking, washing up, preparing food, tidying, always doing something, it doesn't matter what.

Lyuba shows me our room. The bed has old carvings in the oak. I take a shower on the duckboards in the home-made bathroom. Afterwards I take one of the small striped towels hanging in a row by the door and dry myself. I dry each arm and then work around my neck and down my back and front. I wipe down the fronts of my legs and then lift each leg in turn and work around the feet, between the toes. Then up between my legs and testicles and the hair that grows around them. Strange word, testicles. Ridiculous even, as penis is. But then balls is not right either. In Russian they are eggs, which seems even worse.

There's a wood smell from the deal panelling in the bedroom. A green mosquito net has been tacked over the open window. It's warm and there's no need for a duvet.

Before I doze off Lyuba comes in. I keep my eyes closed as if I was asleep, though I really am half asleep. She turns out the light and I put my arm around her. It takes a while for us to come together. There is a silence that has crept between us. Maybe it was always there, but before it was always broken when I first stretched over, during the first moments of contact. Now it takes longer. Her face is somewhere here though I cannot see in the dark; her hair brushes my mouth. With my hand I trace an outline around her hips, her waist and leg, reminding myself of what I have in my hands, of what my body is pressing against. Then I run my fingers round the curve of her cheek, her ear, and at last sensuality begins to break through, a strange selfishness, as if you might have turned off a control switch and managed to forget for a moment. We struggle for a short while, a ritual fight full of anomalies, gestures of tenderness, imaginings of other erotic moments passing through in the darkness, thoughts of other women, banal thoughts, everything jumbled up, chaotic and without plan. And then the end comes, which I'm grateful for.

5

The sun is pouring through the small window, and even with the small opening it's bright in the room. The sheets glare, like spray in the sun. It's late. Lyuba is curled up, the duvet protecting her form and the round of her small head, like a nest. I can see her nose, a closed eye, a stray wisp of hair.

The cramped bathroom has a good smell of sponges and soap. I pad bare-foot to the kitchen in my khaki shorts. Sleepy. The sun is warm, reflecting off the painted wooden floorboards as off a mirror. I lean against the porch rail that overlooks the pond, squashing my arms against my chest, enjoying the gradual awakening of my heavy body. Olga is picking blackcurrants. She looks through the leaves and drops the small, dark berries into a bowl.

'Nu davai! Prygai!' she shouts, in encouragement.

Miles pushes the inflatable dinghy out from the reeds with his foot and while it is still moving jumps in, landing on his side with his legs spread out behind. The soft plastic buckles but the water doesn't come in, and soon he is paddling over to the further bank into the lilies.

'Why should you leave as soon as you arrive?' Olga asks me.

I look across at the trees.

'I wasn't going to,' I say.

The phone has been ringing and Olga answers, props it in place with one raised shoulder, and picks up the bowl to take inside. I'd mentioned something to Lyuba yesterday, but it was more of a hint than anything else. I'd suggested we go to Crimea with the children, and then said something about the Caucasus because I thought she might enjoy the mountains more than the beaches. Lyuba has told Olga, and now the subject of a trip is out in the open and ready for discussion.

Scraps of conversation come from the kitchen. Olga's talking of how I want to take the children: '...He's thinking of Crimea! And the Caucasus...the *Caucasus!*' She emphasises the names as if they were the sort of places one might think of going if one was soft in the head. She mentions something about accomodation and how difficult it might be to find somewhere to stay. Then she talks of the great heat and how easily Miles burns in the sun.

I walk down the porch steps to the makeshift basketball area, set out with wooden planks and a hoop nailed to the side of the shed. My idea is to bring the children south and have a family holiday of the sort we never used to take. It's quite clear in my head what it could be, the sitting around under raffia awnings by the sea, the glitter beyond the waves, the long lazy lunches. It's a dream of a family coming together in a distant and beautiful place as it might happen in a Wes Anderson movie.

The Crimean beach, where I imagine this movie-styled raffia-shaded lunch, would have occupied the space at the bottom edge of the map on my old bedroom wall, where the Black Sea began. The mountains of the Caucasus were a little to the right, surrounded by an area criss-crossed with peat bog and close to the blue tongue that poked up from the bottom, a place that came alive in my dreams and turned into the face of an old man who urged me to quit or stay until I felt like exploding.

The Caucasus had something to do with turtles. The turtle idea came from Lewis Carrol's *Alice's Adventures in Wonderland* and all the business to do with the Caucus Race and the Dodo that looked like a turtle, or a Mock Turtle, or whatever it was it looked like. The actual land of the Caucasus, according to my first geographical ideas, was somewhere unique. It had a fault line running through it, a huge fault line, worse even than the San Andreas fault, that opened up from time to time and swallowed things. Just as the idea of the turtle had come to me through reading Lewis Carrol, so the idea of a fault, or dark chasm into which you might fall, was formed by newspaper stories and the way commentators and politicians made free with analogies. Whenever conflicts broke out on ethnic lines, there would be 'fault lines'. Sometimes there would be a huge fault line such as that one that split the Balkans apart long ago and caused the first world war. At other times a place would be criss-crossed in fault lines of all different levels of magnitude. Such was the Caucasus.

Later on I discovered Lermontov and was immediately hooked by descriptions of mountains at sunset, and of wild Chechen braves. After finishing *The Cossacks* by Leo Tolstoy, I felt as if I had been there myself and lived through a lifetime of adventures. Olenin became my hero with all his imaginings and all his failings, and the Caucasus became a place one might escape to and lead a life of hunting and fishing and lazing around.

Gradually I added real things to the picture. Lyuba used to talk fondly of her first industrial placement at a steel plant near Krasnodar, on the Kuban River, and recounted stories from the Caucasus that involved neither disillusioned noblemen and ambushes with Chechens, nor the manly pastimes of hunting and fishing. She told me of her mother's family who used to go on holiday there. In her flat in Moscow she ran rolls of eight millimetre colour film on an old projector. The home movies showed her grandparents playing badminton in the grounds of a mountain sanatorium and later, in the noisily-flicking half-light, a serpentine of healthy looking, short-trousered walkers trekking up a winding path in single file towards the pink, treeless peaks that rose up behind them.

The films reminded me of other films which at one time I had thought dull but which I now enjoyed. They were old Russian classics about gangster life in the southern republics involving abduction and smuggling, films which played on the hot tempered character of the south, where the food was so good and the women so beautiful, and where the drudgery of Communist life was diluted and turned into comedy. In these films the innocent abroad who ran into trouble and became the hero was always the standard Russian. The black-haired villains were the locals, the Georgians, or Circassians, or Chechens, or Abkhazians. Those who spoilt the day were always the party apparatchiks. They were wholly innocent films, and had become very appealing to me.

It will be possible in the time we have to go to Crimea, or to get as far as the Caucasus, but taking the children might not be so simple. It's a long way to travel and questions will be raised as to how we are to go there, whether by car or train, or in some combination with a flight to Krasnodar. The whole thing will be discussed and gone over, and eventually the to-ing and fro-ing will put the children off. They will decide that they want to stay here, and then the old family troubles which I have been trying so hard to avoid will return again, and everything will be back to how it was.

The sound of high pitched screams comes from the road. Then the gate bangs and Daisy and her friend Masha run into the garden barefoot. They have come to play table tennis. Masha has not seen me for a year, Daisy since last night. They wave and then get going, pushing the ball inexpertly backwards and forwards. Their bodies are beautiful and hard, tanned to a biscuity brown.

The sun has gone behind the willows. I follow a path by the side of the pond until it stops in the bushes by a patch of nettles. Then I hang onto the bottom branches of a blackthorn tree, and pull myself up a bank to the edge of an uncultivated field. The grass is rank and tall, and rising above are pale purple spikes of willow herb.

Somewhere here is the last dread spot for all the young children of the village, a place beyond which they will not go without an adult. Fear is confused but bubbling up all the time. Baba Yaga, the witch who lives in the forest in a wooden hut on giant chicken legs, might come crashing through here if you are alone. This witch threat is perhaps the worst of all the threats because it grows so quickly out of nothing and cannot be avoided. And then there is Zhenia. There is something grotesque about Zhenia, a real person who can often be seen walking in the village. When she was young she was kicked in the head by a horse and since then has suffered delusions. She hides her face, wears shapeless, filthy clothes, walks with an awkward stoop. It's hard to know how old she is. She cannot talk well, and has never been to school. She often howls under the telegraph pole where the road divides and leads down to the lake. She must be avoided at all costs. Sasha, the youngest of the gang of friends, stays all summer in a house on the other side of the telegraph pole where Zhenia stands and howls. And so it happens that once in a while - quite often each day - the children need to pass her. If Sasha wants to come over he has no choice. If Zhenia is there he must walk on the opposite side of the road. He mustn't look at her directly and he must be prepared to run if Zhenia turns to talk. He must not show that he's scared and shaking.

And yet Zhenia is really just a stinky old woman. If you are young you can run easily from her. There are worse threats. There's the dog in the garden with the tall fence, the one that rushes over every time you come near. Every day on the way to the lake you pass by this fence, and this dog. And each time you pass, the dog runs across with the intention of tearing your throat out, hits the fence with its front paws and begins a long, low, blood-curdling growl.

Sometimes the scariest thing of all is the forest. Just the look of it is enough to send shivers down your back. Even in the daytime. You might walk as far as the rubbish bins past the last house in the village, and out into the open fields. The sky is empty, tiny birds with tiny voices fly high, lost in this great space. An empty road, and over there the forest. Dark. Silent. Suddenly you are gripped by fear, worse than all the other fears, worse than the dog with saliva dripping from its blood-red mouth, worse than Zhenia, worse even than Baba Yaga. The forest – it's enough to send you running back home, your heart pounding, hoping and praying that you might be good, that your friends will be there when you arrive, that there will be pancakes, grandmother, sok to drink...

I walk back towards the house from the other side of the pond. The fence that is broken is just beyond the tall reeds. The gap is hidden from the road, but it's not good to leave without mending it. In these villages the population dwindles to practically zero during the winter months. If somebody sees a fence lying flat it would give them half an excuse to come into the garden, and once in the garden it's only a short step to breaking open a window and looting everything that can be found.

Across the road is a concrete block barn with a metal door which is used as a lock-up over winter. Everything moveable from the house is stored there and then taken out again by Nikolai when he returns in March. This year he wasn't able to come so soon and the garden was left to grow wild. In normal circumstances he would have mended the fence by now. That was how he spent his time here. For the first few weeks he would concentrate on the garden, digging and planting. Then came the improvements. Every year a new project was begun, a bore hole sunk, a pumping system for the shower installed, a hot water tank fitted, books and furniture salvaged from the old dacha closer to Moscow, a climbing frame put up.

Last year he dug a new camp-style toilet. For a long time, he resisted. He didn't think it necessary: 'Zachem?' he asked, his eyes wide open, the wrinkles on his forehead rising up in an expression of shocked surprise. Olga wanted him to do it but didn't care to let him see this. They met in the kitchen. Nikolai sat down with a mug of black tea and stared at his wife. The look of studied surprise was written all over his face, but as an act of defiance it no longer worked. He followed her with his eyes as she re-arranged the packets on the sideboard, wiped crumbs, moved dirty glasses towards the sink, swept the floor with the help of a long handled plastic dustpan, refusing to answer him.

The old system (a bucket in the shed) had been the basis of the kucha. All the houses in the village had a kucha. This was the old Russian way. You emptied the shit over a patch of ground and come spring you spread it over the garden. A kucha would last three years or so, and then it would be moved to another patch. And so the whole garden was fertilized in the old way, by everybody. This is what village people did, how they'd always prepared their gardens. But Olga didn't like the bucket. The thought of emptying it made her feel sick - and the children hated it too.

Nikolai complained and put it off, but in the end he wasn't given a choice, and so he began digging at the bottom of the garden. Olga watched from the window as he slogged away in his shirt sleeves. He fought the light sandy earth with resentment, sinking ever further down until he disappeared from view. You wouldn't have known he was there except for the odd spadeful of soil shooting upwards.

The new toilet sits on top of the hole like a sentry box. It's built very solidly out of fresh-cut pine boards, with cracks at head height so light can enter. Inside there is a wooden bench with a hole in the middle. A place to settle down for a while, and ponder nothing in particular. Pasted on the rough wood door directly opposite the plank where you sit is a double page spread from a magazine with photos of a collectable china doll, the sort of children's doll which might feature in a horror film as the incarnation of broken innocence, or else in a thriller as the cynical hiding place for an assassin's bomb; a substantial doll in which one might plant something really lethal. It stares at you in various poses – decked out in traditional Russian costume, in a ball gown with muffler and pearls, and completely naked so that you can see every detail of its hard, glossy body. You have no choice but to stare back. If you do not want to reflect on its weird innocence you must shut your eyes.

I walk across the garden in bare feet and, because my pale skin is not yet toughened up, every stone and twig digs into the flesh. Young nettles brush my ankles. The ground around the vegetable beds is soft, and gives way under my heels, rising up between my toes like sand. There is a raised porch to the house where you can lean on the balcony and look back over the garden and that part of the unmade road that can be seen beyond the fence, the neighbour's house set back from the road, and the group of aspens that are not yet tall, with spots across their pale grey trunks.

The village is quiet. Just the sort of place of no consequence that always gets forgotten by the outside world. The children are off somewhere while the grandparents keep things in order, clean, cook, deal with household chores. The young people back from Moscow laze around. Nikolai's radio plays in the kitchen all day on Ekho Moskvy. Something has happened in the Yamal peninsula, beyond the Arctic circle, a mystery event that has left a crater in this remote Siberian place. An enormous black pit that is too dangerous to approach has been photographed from an airplane.

The peninsula is two thousand kilometres away, a place of natural gas reserves and herds of reindeer that cross the tundra migrating to their seasonal feeding grounds. In winter the herds move south. In the spring they cross the still-frozen Ob River to wander as far as the shores of the Kara Sea. It's further from here to Yamal than it is from here to London. Yamal is an end-of-the-world region associated with strange happenings. London is seen as a hotbed of intrigue, and the young people back from Moscow regard me with caution. The troubles of the world are filtered through the radio and television, and everything foreign is piled up in a big heap off to one side, not to be trusted.

Some years ago I was trying to get through to Lyuba on the phone. Wildfires had spread across Russia and air travel to and from Moscow was restricted. Record summer temperatures and long months of drought had dried up the fields and scrub around the forests, and once the fires began they ran out of control very quickly. I was visiting my aunt in Toronto, where it was also hot. She had a habit of watching different screens simultaneously on her television with the volume turned up full because her hearing was poor. It was dark in the flat, with long-tendrilled Chinese ferns blocking the light that would have otherwise have come in through windows that were shut. Her husband had his own flat above her living quarters, in a lighter, tidier place overlooking the lakefront. When I tried calling Vashutino I would hear laughs from the old English comedy shows he liked to watch, competing with the news channel that ran on my aunt's television. I stood in shorts and flip-flops by the fridge, leaving messages with a phone service I wasn't sure still worked, and looking through the open door to the living room at a world that seemed to have caught fire everywhere at the same time. There were fires in Greece and in Portugal. California was in flames. Australia had been in flames and would soon be again. When it came to Russia, the television showed a sequence of pictures over and over, long still images of a hazy Moscow street, followed by pictures of a field engulfed in smoke, a few erratic flames flickering in the scrubby grass but hardly visible in the sunlight, and a line of people putting out fires with what looked like garden rakes. My aunt was following the trial of Charles Taylor, the former dictator of Liberia, who was being charged in Holland with crimes against humanity. Naomi Campbell was summoned as a witness, and in her opening statement she said that before receiving a pouch of dirty stones in the middle of the night, from two unknown men who broke into her hotel room, she had not heard of Charles Taylor, nor even of Liberia. When the prosecution asked if she knew the stones were diamonds she looked frightened and very beautiful, and said she didn't know that either. There were pictures of Monrovia - which wasn't in flames - and then of the court in The Hague. Then we were back to the haze-filled Moscow street, the people raking the fires, and somebody explaining how children and old people were prohibited from leaving their apartments. Fires had begun in Kazan, and to the south in Voronezh. Beyond the Urals they had spread down from Yekaterinburg. Still further east there was a huge smoke cloud over Lake Baikal. The nuclear facility at Sarov was under threat, and the government was preparing to call a state of emergency.

When at last I managed to get through, it turned out that Vashutino was okay. It was not even smoky, though questions needed answering and Olga was undecided. Should people take one shower a day, or might they be allowed two? Perhaps the whole family could be encouraged to wash with buckets of water? Was it wise to use water from the well to water the potatoes? Should Nikolai continue to allow the neighbours without a well to take water from *his* well to water *their* potatoes?

The pond had shrunk badly even though there was a village-wide ban on drawing water from it. Lyuba told me on the phone of the caked and cracked flats of mud surrounding the landing stages, of rotten, previously submerged logs that had appeared above water, and of her favourite reeds that were wasted and ugly, their pale stalks lying flat in the dirt.

Now it's sunny but not so hot, and in Vashutino those memories of fire have receded. The pond in the garden is up to normal levels again. One of the old willows has fallen and small shoots have started to spring skywards from the half submerged branches. Under the water, soft new roots are already trailing down to the mud at the bottom.

Only Nikolai keeps on about the water situation. He says the well is not deep enough and can't cope, and has set rules about showers and washing up. He's tied a muslin rag to the tap in the kitchen and tells Olga that she should stop using water unnecessarily. The rag helps control the savage flow from the cheap pump, but its real job is to filter out sand. Traces of sand wash through, but not every day. Olga is fed up, tells him to stop messing around, and says that life is becoming unbearable. It's as if he wants to find sand there. She used to leave the tap running when she washed up, but now that she's following Nikolai's strict new rules a pile of greasy plates keeps growing. Big, black flies arc slowly over the sink where the muslin rag hangs like a scrap of soiled underwear. A kind of equilibrium has settled in the air.

6

For some reason I find myself thinking of the old war film *Bridge over the River Kwai*. Maybe it's the brightness of the sun, or maybe I'm identifying with the obtuse, inflexible hero, the British army officer who refuses to work. To prove his point the officer stands ramrod straight for six hours at a stretch until he faints in the Malaysian heatwave, then he's put in a corrugated tin pen for a day or so. Why does his position remind me of my position? Maybe it's the army shorts I'm wearing, or my Englishness in this pool of Russianness. The officer's determination always seemed to me both admirable and silly in equal quantities, but then that was often the way with English virtue: honourable determination, followed by a noble failure. You cannot imagine a Russian war movie like that. In Russia, virtues are less abstract, more focused. Heroism is always linked to specific events, to promises, to love.

I'm shaving in the garden next to the table where the plates are left to dry. It's a long time since I've washed outside. The mirror is propped on a shelf next to the soap and a cup of toothbrushes, and it reflects the hard, empty look on my face very clearly against the bright sky. Willow leaves sway all together like a living curtain between the garden and the pond. A crow flies by with uneven, laboured wing beats, and lets out a single shriek: 'Khaaaaaar!' I push the metal stopper on the hand-washer with the back of my hand and douse my face and neck until the soap is rinsed off.

Wild thyme rises over the resinous scent of lavender. A mosquito lands on my arm. I squash it before it has time to settle and instantly there is a scene of devastation, legs, body, head – all mashed chaotically together. A streak of bright blood describes the impact precisely.

Lyuba is still in bed, Olga is making breakfast in her dressing gown. The children have asked for shariki (little balls), a name they use for lenivye vareniki, a kind of curd cake that is simmered in boiling water. There are fresh eggs, black bread, kolbasa (Russian sausage), pirozhki over from yesterday (pasties stuffed with cabbage and chopped, hard-boiled eggs). Yesterday Olga made syrniki. She used fresh curds, the same as she's using for the shariki now, except she added sugar and currants to the mixture. Then she moulded little cakes and fried them until they turned golden brown. These syrniki are like sweeter, softer versions of the Welsh cakes my grandmother used to make.

The children are standing around in a tall way, waiting, moving, keeping their eyes on the ingredients that are spread over the kitchen surface, the curds, the open pack of flour, the broken egg shells.

'How many?' Olga asks from the cooker, spoon in the air.

'Fourteen,' Miles says

'Really – fourteen?'

'Twelve,' says Daisy, with a conscious effort to appear sensible.

Olga nods her head sagely and repeats 'twelve' in a sing-song voice, as if she was finishing off one of her Jewish prayers. Then she cuts up the curd mixture that has been rolled and dusted with flour and plops the little pieces into the hot water where they immediately begin to move around like dumplings. They are left to simmer in the small aluminium saucepan over the gas until they rise to the top. There they float unsteadily for a short while before being ladled out into bowls, each pile accompanied by a spoon or two of 'water', this again being measured carefully out according to individual taste. While the bowls of shariki are being ordered, I brew a pot of freshly ground coffee. Sour cream is mixed with normal cream, and put on the table. There is blueberry jam, cheese, black bread, butter, a smoky fat-strewn salami.

After breakfast the children go their separate ways, Miles wanders outside to shoot baskets. Daisy returns to the bedroom. It's a quiet time. The children across the road are doing their homework. Sasha might come here to do his piano practice with Alya. I go to the bookshelves. It's dark and cool in this old part of the house and there's plenty of stuff, stacks of papers, photos, old diplomas, maps. Most of the books come from Olga's family dacha in Bolshevo, close to Moscow, and just by looking at the titles you can trace the story of Russia. Here is the stagnant end of Communism, a story of alcoholism and ennui, of long summers of absurdity, and winters that hasten death. A gothic thriller written in 2001 sits next to the childhood reminiscences of Gorky. There are the famous exiles and the famous poets who were handled with strange care by Stalin, then accidently mauled. On a separate shelf are old school text books.

My papers are in a neat pile, but without any order. There are a lot of entries, separate, unconnected pieces, a line drawing of men with beards hauling a barge through a landscape that looks like the Norfolk Broads, a scribbled melody in a minor key with a heave-ho bass, then a separate entry: *Marx was the greediest man who ever lived!* Well, it may be true, but have I got the patience to prove it? A note on my first exposure to Tolstoy: *At fourteen I fell in love with Anna Karenina. At the same time I fell in love with Levin, though I wouldn't have said so then.* Or: *When I first heard a record of David Oistrakh playing the Tchaikovsky violin concerto I said to my father: 'How come it seems as if the orchestra is playing from a long way off?' He told me that Russian music often conveys a sense of endless space.*

When I was sixteen an obsession with Nabokov began that continued into college. *Lolita*; a virtuoso book. I used to like the way he gave the impression of openness, or let's say frankness, of disclosure. In *Lolita*, Nabokov talked of the narrator's predilection for a certain type of girl, of Lolita's precursor, a girl whom the narrator had made love to on a beach in France many years previously. In my notes I also set out the 'precursor' to Lyuba, more strange, more poignant than Nabokov's creation.

Forty years ago I was in the north of England following my mother on one of her working trips for the music board. We stayed in B&Bs, and while she took exams I went for long rambling walks. One day we arranged to meet in the house where she was working that week, an old manor set on its own in parkland. I remember a drawing room where a huge coal fire burned. It was November, late in the afternoon, and through the tall windows I could make out a line of trees that followed a long drive all the way to the road. The door opened and a maid came in with a silver tea tray. She wore a pinafore, a black three-quarter length dress, and a linen cap. She had dark hair and white skin, and when she smiled her teeth looked stained, as if they had been touched with ink. It didn't bother me. I thought she was the most beautiful girl I had ever seen.

Afterwards, when we sat down to dinner, my mother told me that she was Russian, which in those days in England was unexpected. It seemed strange that she had been wearing the costume of a servant from Victorian times, but it was still more odd to find that she was from Russia. I thought of her afterwards as one might imagine an ideal, or something not quite real. Then years later (when Lyuba was having her teeth whitened), I remembered the Victorian-Russian maid's face again, the bad teeth, the old and lonely house, and wondered what had become of her, and if there was a pattern to things that is only ever partially seen, or that you can see only if you look very closely between the lines and from a place where you have forgotten almost everything.

I pick out a heavy volume of Prokudin-Gorsky photographs. Somebody has bookmarked a faded image of the Rostov kremlin with a postcard of Rostov as it is now. Rostov is a small town twenty kilometres from Vashutino, a place of domes and whitewashed walls. I was there last year. The museum had just opened and you could check out all the rooms in the monastery, the murals, the magnificent gold altars.

The cloudless sky has turned all-over white in the picture. A ghostly blank covers most of the lake, grass shows an acid green beneath the treacle-brown of monastic walls. Gorsky was one of the pioneers of colour photography, and Nicholas II, the last Tsar of Russia, was a big fan. In a moment of enthusiasm he ordered a train to be equipped with a dark room and a permit allowing it to be hitched and unhitched at a moment's notice. Gorsky was to have the freedom to make a complete record of the Russian empire in all its diversity. There was no political agenda behind the project. It was the whim of a young prince interested in the latest technology and hoping to create a kind of super-photo-album for the general good.

Fifty years earlier Karl Marx had printed his *Communist Manifesto* in London. The pamphlet-sized book quickly became linked to the working men's cause all over industrialised Europe. A vision of a Native-American paradise set amongst factories, it described a world crammed full of all the exact same stuff as before, except that in this new world nobody owned anything. It was a world that was going to make people happy. More importantly, it was a world that was destined to arrive, that would grow out of the selfishness of the old world through the natural workings of historical inevitability. Every decade brought new translations, new printings. In Europe and America the unions grew in strength and certain concessions were won. But in Russia the government was moving away from liberalism and reform, and as the workers began to request rights so the authorities became more rigid, beating down the first shoots of rebellion with no thought for the damage this caused.

By the time Nicholas II took over, in 1896, people had begun to talk of a real sense of an end. An overwhelming public discontent strained the existing order to breaking point. Strikes were organised on a scale never seen before. Millions of workers downed tools, and the impending doom was likened to the coming of a great flood, or to an apocalyptic, mythological invasion from the east.

Nicholas was said to be a fatalist. He was also keen on tennis and extremely polite. His personal diary reveals a man who was partial to chopping trees. He spent day after day cutting them down and then chopping them up. In the evening he read aloud to his family. He saw the troubles that were ravaging his country with dismay, but also with a detachment that people couldn't understand. This detachment never left him completely. In June of 1917, after the Allies had refused a request from Russia to make a separate peace with Germany, while demoralised Russian troops collapsed in a slow-motion defeat across Poland, Estonia, and Romania, and while a groundswell of public opinion inside the country was preparing to tear down the fabric of Russian life, to eliminate class, and to put society, all society, into chains, he gathered his family around in the drawing room of his palace in Tsarskoye Selo, and read them *The Count of Monte Cristo*.

In the story (Dumas's story), the hero has been unjustly thrown into jail (into a French island jail which we must imagine as being one of the worst jails in the world). He is befriended by a fellow inmate, an old man, who tells him of a secret treasure. The old man dies but not without giving his friend, the Count-to-be, a means of escape. The hero swaps places with the dead man and is thrown to the sharks in a body bag. He wriggles out at the last moment and swims to freedom. Later he finds the treasure.

He returns to Marseilles and then to Paris, unrecognised and fabulously rich. He reinstates his ruined benefactor, takes terrible revenge on his accuser, and uses his enormous, almost infinite wealth to destroy all his enemies. He destroys them as a poker player with too many chips wipes out everybody else at the table.

It's a very Russian scenario. Maybe Nicholas felt a kinship with the fictional count. He couldn't have known what was in store for him and his family, but he might have sympathised with the power of unlimited wealth, and with the cash-rich nobleman who wielded tremendous charisma and took revenge. Nicholas wasn't, after all, particularly charismatic by contemporary accounts. He was shy and retiring. He collected mechanical toys. He was criticised for being detached and unemotional, and he resented these criticisms. He imagined it was just how he appeared, but that inside he was passionate and engaged.

And yet the things people said were all true. During the period of his house arrest he spent most of his days outside with his family chopping trees. As the situation in the capital worsened his advisors and his guards warned him to stay indoors. They told him that the crowd was 'ugly', and that they feared for his safety. Nicholas was not put off in the least. He set out with his axe, wearing a buttoned up white jacket with a leather belt pulled in tightly round his still-thin waist. Just near the park where he liked to work was a public road, separated from the palace grounds by a low metal fence. People knew he came here, and they would gather to watch. Now they were watching an exhibit that was soon to be auctioned off, or better say, removed. They were watching a slice of history as it tumbled off the edge of a precipice. One of those rare moments. Perhaps it was mesmerising. Nicholas said he didn't mind being watched, laughed at, having bits of debris thrown at him by a baying crowd. That was his nature. Fatalistic. Kind. Not a struggler. Not a leader of people.

There are no photographs of Nicholas in Prokudin-Gorsky's book. No pictures of angry crowds, striking workers, political speeches, rabble rousers or government troops. No generals on horseback. Instead there are rivers and railways, forests, churches, school children in national dress, locals smoking on the steps of their houses, old bent men, stiff lines of villagers, captains of ships, aloof monks, aristocratic dreamers. Everybody welcomed him and smiled. War in Europe had not yet broken out, and all those monstrously fat wives described by Herzen seemed to have groveled shamelessly to him. Gorsky was the Tsar's friend. A beam of light had travelled across the great provincial wildernesses and reached them as if by a miracle. A snatch of conversation, or simply a stray glance, was enough to draw them closer, to make their lives seem suddenly worthwhile and wonderful.

There is a picture of Gorsky, a self-portrait sitting by a Siberian river. The urbane, suited photographer, reclines on a rock. Behind him is a backdrop of pine forests and mountains patched with snow. He wears a hat and carries a strong stick. He has a beard and glasses and a quizzical expression. The river is not wide, but it runs fast between big boulders. Where the current breaks over the half submerged rocks the water looks silky, and the long exposure time gives the photograph a heavy weight of belonging to a period. Otherwise it shows a landscape that doesn't change, that probably looks the same now as it did then, a wilderness of lichen covered rocks, small spring flowers, dead and bleached twigs, iron-bearing stones rounded out by the water, bone dry and pale in the sun, and red-brown in the current.

There are two more portraits near the front of the book, two famous ones. The first is of the Emir of Bukhara, taken when Gorsky was traveling through Uzbekistan. Gorsky doesn't seem to have had any problem processing the colour in this one. The emir is wearing a voluminous and padded silk dressing gown, cornflower blue with yellow lilies and irises woven arabesque-like into the design. A gold sword is buckled around his middle. His leather boots are pointed, high-heeled, extremely shiny. His expression is soft, his pudgy face set a little to one side, the large square beard pressed against the collar of his dressing gown. He looks fantastically foreign, the last representative of the southernmost outpost of the empire.

The last major portrait, and the most famous of all the pictures, is a portrait of Tolstoy. A letter from Gorsky is included in the commentary:

'*Respected Leo Nikolayevich,*

Long ago I developed a colour photographic plate on which someone took your picture (I forget his name). The result was not good, likely because the photographer was not well acquainted with his craft.

Photography in natural colours is my speciality and it is possible that you have seen my name in print. After many years of work I have finally achieved an excellent transfer of images in true colour. My colour projections are well known in Europe and in Russia. The process of photography according to my method takes 1-3 seconds, and so I have taken the liberty of asking your permission to visit you for a day or two, bearing in mind your health and the weather, so as to take several colour photographs of you and your wife.

I think that in reproducing you in true colour in your usual surroundings I would do the whole world a great service. These images are eternal; they do not change. Nothing rendered in paint can achieve such results...'

It was 1907 and Tolstoy had just turned seventy-nine. On receiving this letter he declined to answer. Then he relented, going as far as to suggest that his wife might like to be photographed. The following morning he changed his mind once more, and agreed to pose.

He was photographed just after his afternoon horseback ride, sitting on a cane chair in the grounds of his estate at Yasnaya Polyana. His legs are crossed angrily. He wears high, hand-made leather boots, and a peasant smock. Behind him, between the trunks of tall trees, the sun pours through the informal gardens.

The photograph did exactly what Gorsky promised; it eternalised an image of the great man as he must have appeared to those around him: an unhappy prophet, unable to conquer his own shadow.

In the summer of 1907 Russia was poised between revolutions, and between wars. The almost-full-blooded revolution of 1905, that set the stage for what was to come, had been ushered in following Russia's defeat in the war with Japan. The 1917 revolution was bound up with Russia's defeat in the first world war. At this interim point, after the first warning contractions of the catastrophe that was soon to arrive, and at almost the exact moment that Tolstoy was captured on film pondering the discrepancies and problems of life in his beautiful garden, a group of ambitious gangsters headed up by a youthful Stalin, known amongst his circle of firebrand revolutionaries as Koba, carried out one of the biggest and most dramatic bank robberies ever seen in Russian history. Forty people were killed by a bomb on the main square in Tiflis. Three hundred thousand rubles were stolen in broad daylight, and Tolstoy's famous message of love suddenly became entirely irrelevant.

7

Daisy is hunched in the back of the car, painting her nails with a pot of black varnish she has just bought in the market. The nails are coloured alternately so they look like piano keys. Later, when she meets up with Masha, they will sit down with the rest of their colour collection and add details, faces, eyes, little hearts. Miles sits awkwardly, his body pushed to one side as far as he can from her, his head leant out of the window in disgust. Daisy looks up for a moment.

'What's your problem, pig?'

'It stinks! Mama! Tell Daisy to wait until we get home.'

We are returning from Pereslavl with food shopping, including some packets of sukhariki, a kind of broken up toast with a salty tang that Miles asked for.

'I'm going to die! Mama!'

'Get a life, pig!'

Miles is wearing aviator shades with gold rims, also newly bought in the market, and he is acting as if the end of world had just arrived. At the turn-off for Vashutino, Lyuba turns and tells them to be quiet. Then she announces to us all that Nikolai has cancer and that Baba is going with him tomorrow to Moscow for a consultation.

The children go quiet, but it doesn't come as such a shock to me. There was a skype session earlier in the year when I noticed a difference in his face. It looked long where before it had been broad and fleshy, and his eyes were in shadow, whereas before they had been ready to smile behind creased cheeks.

Three years ago it had been Olga with cancer. That had been the first heavy blow since my father died. Olga survived a mammoth operation, and now her hair has grown back, and she looks silver-grey healthy.

When we get back Olga is in the kitchen and Nikolai is in his room. Outside the new fence posts are lying by the raspberry bushes.

Olga has arranged for one of her old friends to come and stay with the children while she is in Moscow with Nikolai. She wants Lyuba and me to go off somewhere on a trip, a kind of present for us. She expects us to go south, to the Caucasus perhaps, but without the children.

An iron bar and a holer have been left against the wall inside the tool shed. I clear an area where the old fence is lying flat on the ground, and begin where Nikolai has left off. He has gone down about a foot in three places. There are five new posts to put in, metal ones with lugs welded on to take the cross pieces. The posts are tall and the holes will need to be deep to get the position of the lugs right.

I set to work with the iron bar, picking out stones and roots. It soon becomes clear why Nikolai has stopped where he has. The big stones are hard to lever out, and the holer keeps on getting stuck. Sweat begins to run down my back, and into my eyes. It's slow work, but by lunchtime I have two holes done and rest for a while under the apple tree. Lyuba has prepared svekolnik, a cold soup with fresh dill, shredded beetroot, and a sharp tang of squeezed lemon. It's served with a hard-boiled egg and a dollop of cream. When you break the egg the red of the beetroot leaks into the white flesh and the yellow of the cooked yolk.

I open a cold beer from the fridge and plan the afternoon's work. There's an open bag of cement in the shed and a weedy pile of sand on the road, just outside the gate. Enough to concrete the posts in place.

I haven't asked Miles to help. He's gone with the rest of the kids to the lake to swim. I'm not in the mood to be bossing around, to be laying down the laws of responsibility. If I get on with things then maybe it will be enough to set an example. But even that doesn't seem like such a great idea for the moment.

Olga and Nikolai have gone to the station to pick up the old friend who is going to help with the children while I am supposed to be going with Lyuba for a separate mini-holiday. They left a half hour ago. Lyuba comes out and starts weeding the flower bed.

I move down the bench and into the shade again.

'So, what's happening?' she asks finally.

I want to finish these posts, but for the moment I can't see further than this. Olga's holiday plan seems all wrong to me. The news of Nikolai's cancer is working through us, dredging up all sorts of unfinished business. Thoughts of where he will go and of what we should do, keep knocking up against thoughts of how things could have been different, and how we might have done things better. I can't find anything to say.

'I should make something for when Nadya comes,' Lyuba says.

An apple falls off the tree, makes a small thud, bounces on the grass and rolls to join other small bruised and uneaten apples on the ground. I pick up the holer and put it in the shed. Then I put the open bag of cement into the wheelbarrow and take it to the first hole. By teatime, four posts are in place and the whole gang of children have arrived back from their swim. Olga is chatting to her old friend in the kitchen, and Nikolai is with them. Lyuba is making Napoleon cake, a Russian version of millefeuille, and Daisy has gone next door to borrow some condensed milk.

I open my current book, *A Little Corner of Hell*, and settle down to read on the sofa-bed while supper is prepared.

8

Forty yards or so ahead, the double rear lights of a parked car glow in four circles, two small rings and two large, fully-lit discs. It's dark and late, and I'm trying to keep awake.

It hasn't been a great day. But perhaps it's better now than it was an hour ago. The children have been caught in the invisible tangle of grownups' difficulties. They feel the problems, they understand, and they rebel. Their rebellion consists in judging our adult silliness. The grownups are weak and despicable for making scenes and for being unable to extricate themselves from a problem.

The morning was wasted before it began. I woke late, after a bad night, and with a feeling of nothing resolved. I turned to Lyuba and suggested we ask the children if they wanted to come with us. She nodded but I don't think she heard. When I sat down on Miles's bed in my pyjamas I tried to put as much fun into the proposal as possible.

'What do you think?' I said.

He looked at me while I spread Nikolai's old map of the Soviet Union onto the bed, and traced a line with my finger northwards.

'We could take the road to Arkhangelsk,' I said.

Then I drew my finger up to the broken line of the Arctic Circle.

'Well?' I asked him again.

He seemed to warm to the idea. Daisy wanted to come too, and a little while later we all left in the car. The problems began before we got to the main road. Lyuba decided that a trip together was a bad idea and asked me to turn around. Then, on the way back to the dacha, she became embarrassed. This time she couldn't work out what to do, having already explained to Nadya that we were going to take the children, and having also said goodbye to Alya across the road. So we set out for a second time.

At Vologda we bought a tent, a barbecue, some lighting fuel, and an axe. It rained and the light began to fade. We had another argument. It was too late to turn back and there were no camping places, so we took a side road along the river in the twilight, a meandering road lined with broken cars, and broken houses with broken windows. I kept hoping for the fields to open up and for a place to pitch a tent, but the further we went the worse it became. In the end we turned back to the highway, and drove until we came to a layby in the forest. Here it was boggy and mosquitoes were biting. You could hear the cars, and it felt even less safe than the place by the river. We started off once more, took the next turn-off, and found what seemed to be an empty parking place for lorries. This time Lyuba stayed in the car, while I put up the new tent in the dark with the children.

Now they're asleep. Or at least they're in the tent and I'm here keeping watch. A car has pulled up ahead with its tail lights glowing. Other cars have come by, parked, stayed for a while and left. But this one hasn't left. I turn the lights on, then turn them off and wait. It's been a long drive, and I'm nodding off. The barbecue skewers are hidden under the seat, a dangerous weapon maybe. I've slipped the cardboard-wrapped axe under our bags in the boot. Since this car turned up thoughts of violence have never been far from my mind: defence of the family, a blind attack, to get hurt, to hurt someone. How hard to hit the person? If I get into the tent I will be at a disadvantage. Now I just have to keep awake.

The little dynamo of fear keeps working, storing up energy, finding a release. Did they see Daisy earlier when we were putting up the tent together? There were certainly cars which turned near to us, raking our little camp with their headlights. Probably they are interested in both women, the younger and the older. I have no weapon, but bare hands might be just as effective. The last time I fought was in school, and even that wasn't a great success. I didn't want to hurt the other person enough, but in this case it will be different - if I give myself time. And so it goes on, fear rising up, dying down, and then coming back again. It occurs to me that nothing is working out. The children are unhappy, Lyuba is frustrated, maybe even angry, while I am preparing myself to fight. It's all foolish. A real mistake that sooner or later will need to be paid for.

The twin red lights come on. Still I can't see anybody inside. The car moves, reverses, pulls away. I get out and look at the sky, at the summer constellations scattered messily everywhere. A thousand lights, big and small, a milky blur wiped across very high up. A million stars. More than a million, all joined up without any gap between them. A fuzz of stars, and out of the fuzz a few known constellations. A general darkness freshly washed by the rain. But it doesn't feel so peaceful.

I crawl into the tent trying to make as little sound as I can, unzipping and re-zipping, kneeling on the ground to take off my shoes and socks, and then wriggling into the sleeping bag. I listen for the sound of cars, but there is nothing. What else can I do? My hands are clenched into fists and I release them, resting the open fingers across my legs. Three days ago I arrived and disturbed the peace. I wasn't going to come, then I did. We were supposed to travel south with the children, to visit those places where we were happy, when the future was wide open. My idea to take the children to the raffia-awning beach hut for a long lazy holiday was gone-over and discussed by everybody in Vashutino, including the neighbours. In the end even Nikolai joined in. It didn't take long to see that Lyuba didn't want to go to Crimea, or the Caucasus. It was too far to travel, and we would have been away from her parents for too long. The tangle of family interests tied us to Vashutino. And while the holiday conversations had the appearance of practical plan-making, it began to look as if the backwards and forwards talks were a form of power struggle. A kind of survival of the fittest, but with no winners.

Yet we have come through the first trying moment. Nothing has broken down between us, nothing irreversible or final has been said, though a quietness has descended that doesn't feel as if it will go away easily.

We were going to head south, as far as anyone might go while still remaining in Russia, and then we didn't. Now we're going in the exact opposite direction, as far north as anyone can go. Does it matter? I think about it as I drift off. I see myself falling asleep, as if I'd been hovering over my own body, asking the same pointless question over again until something like a button is pressed, a blank from which nothing more is recorded.

9

When I open the tent flap in the morning and step outside, the first thing I notice is a piece of orange peel. Then a stump of cucumber, shriveled, bruised. The fields are scrubby and neglected. Bushes grow in the ditches and in the distance, on a rise, are three dun-coloured apartment buildings. A car whizzes by. I walk away from the tent to pee, take a deep breath of fresh air, and notice a condom lying in the dew-wet grass. Not far away are more bits of old fruit, cartons, rocks, a bag with a broken handle.

Strange that we set up camp on top of all this last night without knowing it was here. It feels early, and while I fix the barbecue to make a cup of tea I spot another condom. I get a stick and flick it away, and then start looking in case there are more. I kick away the piece of cucumber and the scrap of orange peel, and suddenly realise my mistake. We have stayed in a place used by the young people of the nearby town for their night-time trysts. Those people who stopped with their car lights glowing for so long were lovers, fumbling to undo each other's clothes, while I prepared myself for my murderous attack.

The road is poorly surfaced but wide and straight, and the occasional cars pass by with lots of tyre noise, as if they had punctures. There's a little rush around seven o'clock, and then it goes quiet again. A school bus arrives, turns in the parking lot by the rubbish, waits for a while and then heads back the way it came.

The tea smells of the plastic camping mugs. Miles toasts bread while Lyuba cuts up the cheese. Daisy has taken charge of Nikolai's old map. She reads off the names of towns and villages we are due to drive through. There aren't many. The road follows a river as far as Arkhangelsk, curls around the coast, and then stops.

We pack up the tent, not without some pride at having survived the night. The difficulties that always grow in darkness have gone away, and towards lunchtime we stop by the edge of the river. It's broad and blue with sandy islands and sandy banks.

We are heading for Solovki, but it will take another two days to get there. Solovki is an old island prison camp with a famous monastery on the White Sea. The children like the idea of the White Sea. I have told them that beyond the White Sea is the Barents Sea, that beyond Solovki is Murmansk, and that close by Murmansk are the naval bases, some of them marked on the map and some not, and that it is here that the Northern Fleet is stationed.

10

Nixon was briefed many times before his trip to Russia in 1972. For months there had been backwards and forwards talks with Moscow. Nobody expected the known problems to go away, and yet it had become necessary to talk of them, so as not to miss anything that might be done to steer the two powers on a course that would not end in disaster, or the beginning of disaster that might be averted. While a whole series of letters and communiques between the two sides were issued and responded to concerning the problems of territorial ambiguity in Berlin, the Arab States and Israel, and America's involvement in Vietnam, there was another direction to the discussions that pushed ever closer to the dark centre of the problem that had to do with fears of a nuclear war. A final letter sent to Nixon from Brezhnev outlined a favourable outcome for talks, but it was also laced with threats to ensure a plan was stuck to, with nothing left to chance. The modesty of the proposal was surprising. It was the communication of a blindfolded man walking through a series of known obstacles, checking with outstretched hands before making any move, trying his utmost not to harm himself, or to set in motion an irreversible mistake.

During the week before his flight Nixon watched two films. One of them, *Faces of Russia*, was a propaganda documentary with an anthropological angle made by the Soviets. The day before he left he watched *From Russia with Love*, an early James Bond movie starring Sean Connery.

Air Force One landed in Moscow on the 22nd of May 1972. It was warm and overcast, with rain just holding off. There was a sense of trepidation and of pride on the Russian side, as if they wished to prove the worthiness of their existence, even against their will. Everything was exactly choreographed, the six-strong welcoming party with a perfectly timed walk to the edge of the red carpet, the flags, the guard of honour with their sabres and their shiny boots and caps, the virtuoso rendition of The Star-Spangled Banner anthem, the small public crowd arranged to one side behind a soft rope, the nice-looking woman positioned right at the front with her camera and her free-and-easy manner.

The president emerged from the plane hand in hand with his wife, Patricia. Following them down the Aeroflot steps, one hand clinging to the pink safety rail, was Kissinger, the mastermind of cold war politics, his circular lensed glasses reflecting the light whenever he turned his head.

Nixon was in Russia for a week and according to White House logs he telephoned his daughters twice and his special advisor, Charles Colson, four times. Lastly, he made a telephone call to Billy Graham, who was at that time on an evangelical crusade in Ireland. Billy Graham liked to explain that in the event of a nuclear strike believers would go straight to heaven while non-believers would go straight to hell. This super-violent proposal caused little waves of panic amongst those who didn't believe this would actually happen; for these sceptics the idea that some people were prepared to think in these terms, even perhaps in England, was enough to inspire plans of emigration.

The summit talks were held while we still lived in the quiet commuter town of Chorleywood, just outside London. Every American president was expected to show faith, but the Christianity preached by Billy Graham was viewed by my father as a horrific, contagious disease. One night he came to my bedroom and sat on the edge of my bed just before I turned the light out. He waited a while with his legs crossed and his head propped in his hands, casting a shadow over the giant military map that showed every lake, river, bog, airfield, factory chimney, slag pile, and monument west of Magnitogorsk. We didn't talk much, and I was curious to hear what he had to say. In the end he turned and asked my opinion on whether or not he should take a job he had been offered in New Zealand, at the university of Auckland. He told me that Europe was wonderful, beautiful, but that it was a like a rose that was almost finished, that was beginning to rot. I listened to his elegiac descriptions of Europe and then of his more upbeat descriptions of New Zealand (though these, too, were strangely tinged with sadness). Then I went to sleep with these two images, the decaying rose of Europe and the Anchor-butter optimism represented by New Zealand, competing in my head like two books I needed to choose from.

My father's plans for trans-hemispheric emigration never came to anything, but we did leave Chorleywood. Soon after the conversation in which he likened Europe to a dying rose he took us to live in the old servants' quarters of a rambling manor set in the middle of fields near the village of Chalfont St Giles.

The old military map now hung in my new bedroom and it felt familiar and good. My father did his typing in his own room and you could hardly hear it any more, but it wasn't possible to escape his constant brooding. Worrying about a nuclear holocaust had no end. He shut himself in but you knew he was there, his hands hovering over the keys as he composed his next thought. The fate of the world hung in the balance, while outside our kitchen window a row of cows from the neighbouring farm bellowed non-stop. They had been separated from their calves and were caught in a loop of their own suffering, but it made no difference. It had become clear to me that all suffering, whether of cows or of humans, was the same in the end.

I began to see the world through my father's eyes: Truman was bad because he had ordered the dropping of atom bombs on Hiroshima and Nagasaki. Lenin was good because he had fought and won for the people, the poor people who couldn't fight and win for themselves. Nixon was bad because he used bad language in secret conversations that were recorded, and because he sounded so coarse and shifty. Russia was the underdog, and was therefore good. I knew that my father found defending Russia tricky, and I began to search for common ground in order to plug this weak spot: Russia might be in a terrible mess, but compared to my friends' spotlessly tidy homes our house was also in a terrible mess. Russia was oppressed, and a dark cloud of suffering hung over it, but this was the price you paid for upheaval, and I knew about upheaval, too.

The Cold War had something to do with ideology, but ideology was a slippery thing. Words didn't count for much, after all. You had to look at what was what. America began at the lawns of the White House and finished on a perfectly undulating golf course. Russia was darker, older, almost unknown. From this murky picture emerged certain real people: a beautiful sadness surrounded the slight figure of Olga Korbut as she prepared herself for another faultless win on the parallel bars, or on the mat, her hair tied in bunches, her eyes down. A television dramatisation of War and Peace, with a youthful Anthony Hopkins as Pierre, confirmed our family's view of Russia as a country that combined grand style with profound meditation on the deeper questions of life. I wanted to find out what was really happening there. I spent long hours looking at the towns scattered over my map, all with more or less unpronounceable names, and all full of people who might be thinking of me in the same way that I was thinking of them. The Russian people seemed to be looking outwards, uncomplaining, awaiting their fate.

It was around this time that my father began to worry more about money. He didn't spend much himself but always felt the need to economise. Our habits became the habits of a failed socialist state. We were constantly reprimanded for leaving lights on. Chatting on the telephone was not allowed. Our eating was monitored. Toast was handed out piece by piece at breakfast. The amount of butter was noted. If there was too much it had to be scraped off again, and kept for the next slice. Cream was allowed on our puddings for supper, but always in quantities that made us want more.

My grandmother sent me a book in the post. She had been given it by a member of her congregation and now she wanted to warn me of what was really happening out in the world. The book had been written by a man called Sergei, a tough from one of Russia's orphanages and the leader of a hit squad with orders to target Christians who dared to live under Communist rule. Under orders from Moscow the carefully chosen squad beat up as many Christians as they could find, tortured them, stuffed their mouths with sand, smashed the old believer's heads, and raped their young girls. Afterwards Sergei defected in a dramatic escape to Canada, where he converted to Christianity and wrote the tell-all book. I couldn't understand why this person should be a hero in God's eyes just because he had admitted his guilt. Of course a book was just a book, and could be ignored or forgotten about. But our church-going habits were set in stone and there was nothing that could be done about them. We had to go and listen and sing, regardless of what we thought. I was the opposite of a hero, full of anger, resentment, and growing hatred towards God and the world.

Giles was the patron saint of animals, and there was a painted relief of him over the west door of the flint church in the village. He had a sad expression on his face and his hand, held protectively in front of a deer's neck, was pierced by an arrow. Next to the relief was a medieval wall painting, almost worn away, of John the Baptist holding the infant Jesus in his arms. Opposite this family piece was a pit full of sinners holding up their hands to protect themselves from a swarm of black crosses raining down from above: they were The Damned but there was no mention of The Damned in the service, or in the sermons. We were expected to be merciful, forgiving, understanding, but not fearful. We were not threatened with Hell. Hell was hardly mentioned. And in that sense it was not my grandmother's kind of service.

I suppose it was more my father's kind. Perhaps the stone walls and pillars reminded him of his school where he had always excelled and been rewarded for achievements. He liked the church because it was old, but at the same time there was always something getting at him. He took a high attitude. He felt that the expressions of love and compassion that were repeated on Sunday allowed people to behave like rotters through the week. He thought the prayers were just another way to make up for their day-to-day rottenness, which included accepting the status quo in respect of nuclear weapons. His campaigning on behalf of the anti-nuclear lobby was part and parcel of this. He wasn't a particularly sociable man, but he made himself join the local peace group, and soon he was organising this and that. He wasn't too impressed with the group's abilities, just as he hadn't been impressed by the church's lack of voice, and in the end he hijacked both groups, the peace group and the church. He persuaded the vicar to allow him to deliver a sermon. He chose a busy Sunday, dressed himself in a black cassock and white surplice, and delivered an hour long speech from the pulpit. A new and terrifying idea was presented to the congregation: it seemed their own small and sleepy corner of England was allowed its state of permanent sleepiness only through certain deals and arrangements that were always a hair's breadth away from disaster. He was preparing the ground for a new revolution, smashing his pick into the hard English earth of common sense, and challenging the settled and almost-happy people to the same doomsday vision with which he had begun to fight everyone.

11

In the far north, the ocean has a special lonely quality. The waves that run in from the White Sea seem to come from the end of the world, though in actual fact the coast at this point where Onega Bay and Dvina Bay meet, and where the small group of islands including the island of Solovki lie, is protected from the worst Arctic storms by the hump of the Kola peninsula. Beyond is the Barents Sea and the North Passage, where ice-breakers keep a year-round path open through constantly shifting floes.

The seas are rich in all kinds of marine life, and the land has always been home to small fishing communities that survive in isolation, on the very edges of life. At the time of Andrei Rublev and the great icon painters, when Russia was almost ready to push back the Mongol invaders after two hundred years of occupation, a wandering monk crossed the sea from Belomorsk in a small boat and landed on the stony shores of the largest of the uninhabited islands that run across the mouth of Onega Bay. He brought a friend who rowed off soon afterwards for supplies and did not return. The monk slept amongst the rocks and fallen trees near to the shore. It was Autumn, and the first snows were falling. He whispered to himself, repeating the prayers he learnt when he took orders, to strengthen his resolve. He survived the winter, and in spring his friend returned. During his time alone on the island the monk had a vision of an extraordinary monastery bathed in supernatural light.

He was one of the holy men who lived during a time of great upheavals when much of Europe was still ravaged by plague, a saint who had visions of heaven while fighting off the demons of temptation. He worked tirelessly, sending word of a place that had been blessed by God, and where one might spend one's days in contemplation of the divine.

A monastery was built on the shores where the monk first landed that was to become one of the richest and most important in all of Russia. The island had abundant fish and timber, seaweed was harvested, bees were kept, kilns were constructed to fire bricks, there was a tannery, a foundry, salteries. There was a vaulted library. Bells and cannons were cast in the metal workshop. The monastery flourished, was strengthened, and at last finished to the state which can still be recognised today, with six-feet thick walls and round towers capped by roofs that look like four Mongol helmets, pointed and warlike. It became a fortress-monastery, protecting Russia from the north and nurturing a special pure Orthodoxy.

After the revolution of 1917 the island was overrun by the State, and the monastery sacked. The monks who were not killed in this operation now worked for new masters whose first job was to oversee the removal of all valuables, the ripping out of bells from the towers, the burning of wooden icons and crosses for firewood, and the weighing and boxing up of the gold and silver for melting down in Moscow.

After a few months a prison camp was opened on the island, the first of the Soviet work camps, and one that quickly became known for its violent excesses and crazy brutality. In 1925 the relics of the founding saints were dug up and photographs taken of the bones before they were removed to a museum of curiosities. A year later a fire that started in the accounts office of the new state farm destroyed the ancient library.

Much of the prison labour used to construct the canal between the White Sea and Baltic Sea canal came through Solovki. For twenty years it operated under a form of oppression that was allowed to pursue its own violent course all the way to the end, when it was finally closed in 1939.

After the second world war the islands were used by the Soviet navy as a training ground, and when Communism finally came to an end, in 1991, Solovki became a relic, a piece of history rotting away. But it didn't rot away entirely. Too many people had passed through it, too much suffering had accumulated there, the walls were too thick, and it had become the focus of too many different and bizarre passions.

•••

We are not sure whether there is going to be a boat, or if there is one whether we will be able to buy tickets. Some tourists have already booked their places and are waiting in a new wooden cabin by the quayside. We are outside, sheltering in the porch. It's six in the morning and the rain keeps coming in heavy showers. The sea is grey and taut, like silk, and in the distance you can see the low shapes of the first islands.

The children have serious faces. Lyuba is worried we will not be able to get to the islands in time. Daisy needs to be back to Vashutino for a party to celebrate the arrival of one of her friends from Yaroslavl on Tuesday. If we don't leave on Sunday we will be in difficulties, and Lyuba doesn't want to let Daisy down. Miles doesn't mind one way or the other. It always seems odd to me how Lyuba is so concerned over the children's needs and arrangements, and how she makes so much of their independent lives, but now I am beginning to see things her way. What else is to be done about the sullen hatred which grows inside them, that I can clearly see on their faces? They are still young, and today it will quickly dissipate, but maybe it will not go away completely and then there will be that torn-up love as they grow, full of conflict that is never quite resolved. I have taken them here with the promise of a fine time, all words and good intentions and the expectation of how things should be, and they are beginning to see things as they are.

The rain is coming down hard again, and we have pushed our way into the crowded hut to wait with the others in the hush of expectancy. Here you can see the divisions that people make between themselves, even when the stakes are very low. There are about fifteen people and of these fifteen there are maybe ten who aren't sure what's going to happen. We belong to this camp. Or maybe we are the only ones who aren't sure what's happening; the others may be simply worried without any clear defined reason.

Everybody wears rain gear, plastic capes, hats, wellingtons. There's a woman who reminds me of the adulteress in Tolstoy's short story, *The Kreutzer Sonata,* a character described as 'bursting with energy like a vigorous horse'. She's tall and athletic, yet lazy-looking too. Her big hair frames her striking but not so pretty features, and she wears tight blue jeans, high-heeled boots, and a cowboy hat. She's talking to a young man whose wife sits patiently nearby. The young man is polite and makes only small contributions to the conversation, but his attention doesn't waver for a moment. His wife looks as if she might burst into tears at any moment.

An old-timer walks in wearing a yellow oilskin. He has white hair, energetic eyes, and an obstinate expression.

'What kind of place is this without a timetable?' he asks.

The girl behind the desk isn't going to fall for this old bullying trick.

'Ticket please,' she says.

He roots around in his bag and pulls out a grubby paper. She looks at it, turns it over, looks at it again, and then hands it back.

'This is a ticket... but it's not a ticket for our boat.'

'I'm going to Solovki this morning!' He prods downwards vigorously with a stubby finger, and looks her straight in the eye.

'Our boat's all full up. Your ticket is for the monastery boat. We don't have anything to do with the monastery boat.'

The ticket girl goes back to reading her magazine, turning the pages very deliberately, as if she was completely engrossed in it. The man in the oilskin stands for a while in a dramatic pose by a glass cabinet with postcards propped up inside, but he's been defeated and he knows it.

We are close to a strange repository of Russian history, a kind of preserving jar that contains layer upon layer of hardship and pain. Buried within its layers are endless episodes of cruelty, stupidity and suffering. Prisoners scooped up from the general population on the quota system during the time of the great purges were processed here, in a building not far away. They were bullied and tortured to rid them of all normal human feelings of strength and power.

Afterwards they were transported across the water and used up. They were used under the terms of work planned and telegraphed through under orders from Moscow, and were disposed of in the most cruel ways imaginable to satisfy the appetites of the many guards who had become addicted to dealing out punishment and inflicting pain.

The more you read, the more painful it becomes. You begin to ask yourself how it could have happened. Probably the interrogators, guards, and other overseers were sadists and psychopaths, but where did the authorities dig up all these psychopaths? How come so many of them were available for work all of a sudden? There are pictures in the camp archives, photos of armed men in caps and leather coats, belted and buttoned, with matter-of-fact attitudes and the stern expressions of people who carry sticks and work with animals. There has always been a plea for mitigating circumstances – that behind the man with the stick was another with a revolver. But in all the stories that have survived from the camps there are the divisions between guards, between the greater sadists and the lesser sadists, and the rarer sort who tried to make things easier. And all of the greater and lesser sadists in these stories (those who exercised a choice to be greater or lesser sadists, as well as those who chose to make things easier) undermine this plea which asks to state that no choice was available – not an iota of choice – and that certain men were forced at all times to pursue acts of foul cruelty only by the system itself, or by certain other men, by the camp commander perhaps, or Yezhov, or, God forbid, Stalin himself.

I look around at the people waiting in the damp warmth of this brand new rustic hut. I try to imagine them thrust into positions of authority over helpless, hungry, cold and broken prisoners. The woman who reminds me of the seductress in *The Kreutzer Sonata*, for instance, how would she have fared? Or the husband she is toying with? Would he have turned into a brutal torturer? Would he have been a snitch, saving his own skin? And what of the old man in his yellow sou'wester, the picture of male authority?

The first lot of people leave for the quayside. It's still raining, and I have given my coat to Miles. I'm damp and a dull ache has begun to spread across the muscles on one side of my back. We wait for a further half hour at the back of the queue without tickets until the monastery boat turns up. To everybody's relief it turns out that there is just space. A monk with a straggly beard welcomes us on board, takes our money and writes out two receipts, one for us and one which he puts in a leather pouch hanging from his neck.

The trip to Solovki is supposed to be beautiful according to reports which Lyuba has read online, but it's still early and cold, and everyone is wet. We find ourselves a place in the cabin on a long wooden bench together with the tourists, the pilgrims, the relatives, the simply curious. The children fall asleep immediately. It's only a small boat, a converted fishing boat not very high off the water, and out on deck the waves break around the prow making a continuous hissing over the heavy vibration of the engines. Soon we pass the first islands, treeless mounds, some grass-covered, some bare like huge pebbles.

After an hour the monastery comes into view, low and dark in the distance. I stand in the wind made by the boat's speed, listening to the hiss of the foaming wake that keeps falling away and dissolving in the iron-grey water, and looking at the domes, walls, and ramparts that every convict coming from the mainland would have seen. I make an effort but, however hard I try, I can't imagine what it must have been like for those men taken out of the run of life by 'white hands that were not used to work but were strong and knew how to grip well'. Even for those millions of people who were nabbed in such a way and arrested in quota systems all over the country it was apparently a surprise, something unimaginable, or rather not previously imagined.

During the first pages of The Gulag Archipelago, Solzhenitsyn talks of the otherwise invisible prisons and the entrances to these prisons that were everywhere, practically on every street, places that were invisible because people didn't look for them, inconspicuous doors that led to hell. Arrestees found themselves in the position that the wife of an addicted gambler finds herself in after uncovering the truth, the moment when she discovers that every high street has a betting shop.

Some editions of the book include a map, showing all the prison camps of the Soviet Union, each camp marked by a square. The squares cover the map like a mosaic pattern, and there's not a single part of country that hasn't got squares - all 22 million square kilometres are covered. To keep the great enslavement working it was necessary to create a system where anybody could be arrested at any time. Arrests in the middle of the night were justified by reasons concocted out of thin air, and in the end guilt was based on the idea of original sin. There was no forgiveness, and no mechanism to appeal your innocence once you had been taken.

Some camps were worse than others. Those that have been written of stand out. Kolyma has been fixed by Varlam Shalamov on the general map of suffering laid out by Solzhenitsyn. The White Sea Canal project made Solovki famous, as did the visit by Gorky, who wrote afterwards that the country needed such camps. Over the years a handful of escapes resulted in some sensational claims in the international press that were immediately denied by the Soviets, but in the end these cries of the heart made hardly any more impact than the despairing messages scored into logs by exhausted prisoners that were later found by dockworkers unloading timber in Hull and Hamburg. Nobody cared that much.

Just recently, the Nobel Prize-winner Svetlana Alexievich produced an aural documentary of the mental health of the nation as it has been affected by camp survivors and camp psychology, and it turns out that from this sea of suffering only a fraction of the millions of voices have been heard, the line of dirt washed up on the beach after each tide.

The Polish writer, Mariusz Wilk, talks of Solovki as a place where you might see the whole of Russia in miniature. And perhaps this has something to do with the fact that Solovki is an island. There aren't many habitable islands in Russia. Solovki forms an incomplete wedge at the mouth of the White Sea where it becomes the Barents Sea, a plug in the north just as Crimea is an open plug in the south, to the Sea of Azov.

Distinctions blur, a person can be drawn to a place for one reason and become known for talking of something else. While Mariusz Wilk writes about the general hopelessness of those left over from the camp years, of the unbearable weight of suffering and stupidity and sheer bad luck which seems to have accumulated in this place, there is also the beauty which shines through and becomes the most telling message. It is a beauty of loneliness. Poverty, alcoholism, and corruption frame this beauty, and without them he wouldn't have appreciated the miraculous light, the silence of the north, the discovery of beauty in small things and in slow, inconspicuous things - in the worms and slugs and lichens, and in the silent pools that bear witness in the depths of the forest.

...

The children are still asleep, or at least they have their eyes shut. Miles has his foot on the rail that protects the stairwell. Daisy has folded arms, and has sunk into her hoody. Lyuba's eyes are shut too, but I don't think she's asleep. She has the concentrated look she always assumes on sea voyages, a serious, one-track look. After the incessant rain of the night and early morning, the sun is beginning to show in pale, washed-out lemon streaks of light. I go out again, and the children stagger after me. We watch as the rain-darkened domes get closer. The largest one is half covered in scaffolding.

'Daddy?'

'What?' I say.

Miles can't put his question into words. He stifles a yawn, then relapses into silence.

The boat pulls up at a stone pier, opposite the monastery. We need to find somewhere to stay, but this isn't difficult. Places to stay on the island are all marked on google, with telephone numbers and descriptions. We pick our bags from the pile and walk down the pier to a path that runs along the massive fortress wall made of stones the size of cars, rounded, smooth, interlocked by their natural irregular shapes. Groups of people pause for a moment to look at the stones, or at their phones and printed maps. They wear bright colours, and have walking boots and knapsacks. Some are riding bicycles. The roads are sandy, with paths leading off into the woods. The whine of an angle grinder comes from behind a hoarding by one of the workers' metal cabins.

We book into a chalet hotel, four wooden houses with winding paths between them, flowerbeds, and grizzly-bear rugs in the common parts. We have an apartment on the ground floor. Everything is varnished wood, and through the ceiling we can hear a family upstairs, thumping from room to room as they settle in.

We haven't got long here. If we are to be back for Daisy's party then we will have to leave tomorrow or the day after, though there is still uncertainty with the boat and whether there will be tickets available. The monastery boat doesn't work on the weekend, and the day after tomorrow is a Saturday, so if we wait there is a good chance we might not be able to leave the island until Monday. Then it will be Thursday before we are back in Vashutino.

By the time we leave our room it's past midday. The sun is bright, but low in the sky. A herd of goats wanders up the street and then stops by a house with a sign outside that says Museum. Three men stumble down the road, already drunk, small, tanned, with empty expressions and dirty, torn clothes. Could these be the last of the so-called zeks, or the children of the zeks that Mariusz Wilk talks of, the society that he described and presented as a new form of Russian history? Is it possible that these few hopeless drunks inspired such a great book?

It was often said that the land made the people what they were, that the far-reaching Russian wilderness took away a sense of formality and order, and that the energy of the people was used up in simply getting places, surviving, managing. There was never time for niceties, the rough life was always on show and couldn't be hidden away. In old accounts travellers often write of being repelled by the manners of Russians, of being shocked by the crudeness of their notions.

One of the zeks stops a tourist who's riding a hired bicycle. I can't hear what he says but I see the offence rising quickly in the face of the bicyclist who pushes off in disgust. Probably the zek said something obscene.

Later on we find an airstrip in the middle of the island. There are no planes and no tarmac, just grass and a wooden hut like an old station house next to an area of hardstanding. On the way back we pass a terrace of run-down log houses set on their own by a lake. Washing hangs out. A dog stands at the end of a chain. A toddler is crying, and walking after the crying toddler is a small boy putting a hat on the toddler's head. The toddler pulls the hat off and walks away bawling. The small boy goes after the toddler and forces the hat back on again.

There is nothing unusual about this place any more. Here are the same difficulties Mariusz Wilk wrote about thirty years ago, but watered down, almost gone. They have been supplanted by a wave of tourism, much of it organised by monks. The tourists are everywhere, dressed in fashionable summer shorts and shirts and sandals. The zeks are few, sunburnt, dirty, dressed in greasy jumpers with holes in the elbows, and old track trousers. They cannot afford to leave the island, nor can they get the few construction jobs going because they haven't the necessary skills, nor the inclination to learn them. They are like a race apart, the helpless children left over from the labour camp years.

You can spot them easily, always off-balance, thinking of the next drink, and almost completely ignored by those who have come on their pilgrimages to search the past for its sufferings.

We walk further, carrying one of those printed sheets showing hotels, eating places, monuments, and paths across the island. There are familiar names which we will not have time to visit: Hare Islands, Log Bay, Pine Bay, Filimonova Bog, Golgotha...

We reach a place where there is supposed to be a prison. Many people have come here to see prisons, to feel the significance of what might be left over from the camps. A prison on an island of prisons. But where is this one? There is a brick house with a wood-plank extension on the back. Here is some kind of eating place by the look of it. A room where you can sit down. A woman is cooking and two young girls, probably her daughters, are waiting at the tables.

I ask one of the girls where the prison is.

'It's there!' she says, pointing further into the woods with a big smile.

And so we continue through the long grass, stepping over dead branches until we reach another brick building, an oblong house with an institutional feel. There are rows of small windows with bars. The glass is broken and the shutters hang off. Weeds push through cracks in the concreted yard. Dry grass brushes against the walls. The ground floor windows are high off the ground, but by hanging onto the bars I manage to pull myself up and rest my elbows on the ledge to take a look inside.

It's just dusty. The walls are chipped and broken. There is a further room but it's in shadow and I can't see much. The old prison (built by prisoners) has been cleared many years ago, looted of anything remotely useful and left to rot.

I walk further through the woods to the boggy edge of a lake, where the trees begin to thin out. In the distance the domes of the monastery show dark against the sky, just as they appear on the frontispiece of Mariusz Wilk's book, completing the famous outline of the northern citadel that, on the outside and inside, has now been restored to its pre-revolution state. To me it looks like any other monastery, just as the prison looked like any other neglected building. And then I spot something by the water, a large flat piece of rock, and in the rock a series of marks, the tell-tale gouges of a chisel. The chisel blows have done their job. The top of the rock is gone. A long slab is all that is left, with a profile of chisel marks showing in a neat row where the stone was split. The broken rock has lain here for perhaps eighty years, and is mottled all over with greyish lichen. Somebody has forgotten to tidy it away, or maybe they couldn't because it was too big to move easily. The evidence is startling because it is the only thing left over from all the suffering and pain that is still clear to see. To imagine the Gulag days elsewhere on the island requires a leap of imagination, but these marks are like a fresh wound still open.

I call Lyuba over and ask her to pose. She crouches on the rock and I take a picture of her feet with the water lapping over the chisel marks, and then another one of her looking across the lake with the domes of the monastery in the background.

Photographs of the White Sea Canal construction have always been heroic. In the grainy black and white images, half-starved men unused to hard physical work are driven on by armed guards. You can see the inexpert and exhausted side by side with the more able, tougher men. They are all pushing barrows of stones, or dragging heavy cots without wheels, or hammering wedges and chisels into rocks with mittens and bandages wrapped around their freezing hands and faces. It's a picture of slavery, or of hell. Martin Amis called Varlam Shalamov's extraordinary *Kolyma Stories* the stories of a broken man, and perhaps they are. But now I wonder if there is any worth in writing if you have not been broken, that only then when the life has been smashed out of you will there emerge something worthy of life, and worth bringing into the light.

AUTUMN

12

Russia recedes in the extra-large rear view mirror. Russia keeps on coming at me, unfolding beyond the fly-splattered windscreen. Moscow is another six hundred kilometres away. My grandmother's faith, evangelical and hysterical, would have rebelled. She would have seen the Devil hard at work behind every tree, and I wouldn't have been able to persuade her otherwise.

I pass an un-cleared wreck on the side of the road, twisted incredibly beyond anything you might expect. There's something wrong with the radio. It whines and then screeches, and I can't make head or tail of what is being talked about. I give it a few minutes, and then turn it off.

Lyuba has taken Daisy and Miles back to Vashutino by train. I saw them off and now I'm on my own. They won't come south with me. The children have had enough of prisons and Lyuba is worried about her father. Her concern is enough to keep us all amiable and forgiving, and that's a better deal all round. The children might have wanted me gone but they didn't want a scene, any more than Lyuba did.

On the morning before leaving Solovki we sat in the breakfast bar of the chalet, watching Putin give a consolatory talk to the athletes who were banned from attending the Olympic Games. He told them that it was a shame and that the games would not be the same without them, raising the sense of injustice that has now become the start position for all appeals to countrywide unity: the west attacks Russia in any way it can, while long-suffering Russia remains unbroken.

We all started checking our phones. I found a text from Nick inviting me for a drink. Nick is married to Anya, one of those who receive mimosa blossoms from Lyuba in March. I must have forgotten to tell him that I was leaving, but before I managed to send a reply, Daisy was off her phone and pleading to leave. It had all become fraught, and on the way to the small harbour I insisted we take a look inside the museum. It wasn't much of a place. Old propaganda videos ran on a loop, and pride of place was awarded to a letter from one of the prisoners recommending the healthful properties of seaweed.

Now that I'm on my own it's like waking up after a long sleep. I'm putting everything behind me, and in this letting go, and recognising of things as they are, there's a feeling of liberation. The family holiday was cut short, but there's no guilt. Guilt is when you think you should do something to stop others' suffering, and nobody is suffering because I'm here now. The children are doing their own stuff, and Lyuba will spoil them. There's nobody to explain things to anymore, nobody to persuade. For the first time in a long time I feel as if I'd made the right decision.

I'm going to Crimea, to that particular stretch of sea, because I can't not go there, like a murderer who can't stop from revisiting the scene of his crime. I want to find the line of holiday shacks we stayed in one summer, half a life back. I remember a dusty street and a blue-painted door, not far from the beach. If I sketched the route on the map that hung on my old bedroom wall, it would run south from the purple spread of Moscow to the tongue that used to poke up from under my striped mattress. Then it would turn west, all the way along the edge of my blanket to the Black Sea, and the small Crimean resort town of Sudak. Sudak is the bull's eye, one of those red hearts on a sailor's brawny arm, pierced by an arrow.

The emptiness of the country gives a real physical impression of freedom. Each time I follow the wide open contours of the landscape I get the sense of absorbing information, as if it were there to be read like words across the page of a book. A story is traced across each huge field, along the fringe of dark woods on the horizon, and in the clouds that are poised on the rim of the sky. Old travellers' rules used to carry the same solemn and simple promises: write everything down and listen for the secrets of the country that come from the heart. If you meet a man, then let him talk, let him drink and open himself up. Let him share his life and pain.

The English sailor, Hugh Willoughby, who died in 1553 while exploring the north passage over Russia, passed on instructions to his crew:

'Members of the expedition who know how to use a pen are to take notes so as to record every day of the voyage; they are to note comments about new lands, and the people inhabiting them, about the high and low tides of the sea, about the direction of the winds, about the height of the sun, about the movement of the moon and stars. We should treat every person that comes to us well. We should feed him until he or she is satisfied, give them clothing and set them ashore so that they might encourage others to come to us...'

His last entry in the ship's log was less straightforward:

'We entered a bay which plunges two miles inland. In the bay swam seals and enormous fish, while on land we saw white bears, reindeer, wild swans and other creatures unknown to us. After a week of storms, seeing that it was late in the year and the weather was bad, we decided to stay for winter. So we sent a few of our men south-west to see if they could find any people there. They walked for three days and didn't meet anyone. So we sent out men west, but they also returned with nothing. Then we sent our men in a southeasterly direction, but they, too, returned not having found any people or any traces of man...'

The following year his ship was discovered by fishermen, still stuck in the ice. All the men were dead, frozen solid, and mostly in bed, though some were reported to have been sitting round a table in life-like attitudes, pouring drinks and dealing cards, the victims of a sudden and unexpected calamity.

It will take two days to reach Moscow. For much of the time I am driving through virgin forest, gashed with earthworks that reach as far as the gritty edge of the road. I have Nikolai's old map as a backup, but for the moment I'm using my phone which is plugged into its holder on the dash and loaded up with directions to Olga's flat on Energeticheskaya Street.

Loneliness has crept up slowly and inevitably. There was a time when Lyuba used to concern herself about any form of seclusion, and worry that the children would end up 'growing like grass' if we weren't social enough. Now it seems to me that I've always liked loneliness. There are people I could visit in Moscow, but I haven't seen them for a long time and there would be awkwardness. Olga was always keen on meetings arranged on the spur of the moment. Either people would visit us in London, or we would see them in her flat. Once, when I was in Paris, she insisted I phone a friend of hers, a professor of neurology who was attending a conference there: 'Andrei, it's Steve...' I began, sitting on the bed in a motel room on the outskirts of Meaux. There was a silence. 'Olga suggested I ring...' Finally a deep and uncommitted 'Da,' came from the other end of the line, followed by another long silence. I was like a fan who has plucked up the courage to phone the celebrity he worships, and suddenly finds himself stricken with nerves.

In London, Lyuba would speak to her mother in Moscow nearly every day. Olga spent much of her time on the telephone, and phoning her daughter was just part of the long evening spent phone in hand, going through her address book even as she still talked, looking for the next number to dial. She was uncertain at that time if she would ever leave Russia, and perhaps for this reason she imagined we were both in difficulties, or at least that Lyuba was marooned and far from any helping hand. Olga would send DVDs of films set in exotic palm-tree locations with heroes who owned speed boats and made love to beautiful, tanned women. One of her solutions for what she saw as our joint isolation was a two week stay in a newly finished Russian sanatorium. There we would meet people, she said, and enjoy ourselves. She helped to arrange this break for us during those times of new-found Russian extravagance that were always talked of in the English newspapers. We were in need of a holiday and I remember being excited by the idea.

It was January and we were met at the airport by old friends that Lyuba had known since college days. Tanya was blonde and had large doll-like eyes. Vanya was big and handsome in a feminine way. We had known them when they were first happy together, but now something didn't seem right. The currents of conversation wove backwards and forwards between us all, but never actually between Tanya and Vanya. Something had come between them, and they wanted us to know and not to know, both at the same time.

A mile or so from the sanatorium we stopped in the forest on the side of the road. Vanya cleared a space in the deep snow just beyond the first trees and set up a tin-box barbecue. He was an expert and used only a small amount of dry wood to cook the lamb he had marinated himself and brought in a covered dish. We hadn't seen either of them for a long time and I felt like celebrating in a big way. I wanted to build a huge fire and drink as we used to. We drank, but only a little, and when the meat was cooked and eaten we stood around in the snow quietly.

They dropped us at the gates of the sanatorium, by a red and white painted barrier operated from a hut like a traffic policeman's shelter. We waved goodbye, and were let in to the school-like building, and told to go to reception. Our room looked over the flat roof of the gym, and smelt slightly of mildew. Lists of activities were pinned to a cork board. It was clearly a relic from the old days when workers could win tickets through a lottery system, a place to recuperate according to the psychological needs of the population. I read the invitation to be massaged. Another laminated paper showed a person lying flat on a bed, being worked over by a woman dressed in a doctor's coat.

That evening we shared our table at dinner with three reps working for Hilti, the American tool company. We queued for old-style Russian canteen food, tasteless rolls, hunks of processed cheese, and greasy meatballs served with buckwheat.

The following day we ventured into the forest. It wasn't particularly cold. The snow was melting and the paths were slushy. We skied a bit though it wasn't great for skiing. Back at the sanatorium I spent a lot of time trying to book a massage with the nurse in her doctor's white coat, but something always went wrong. I would arrive either too early, or too late. It was the same with the exercise machine and swimming pool rooms. You needed a coupon to use them and I couldn't work out how to get the coupon. Everything was the opposite of how I had imagined it would be. Lyuba didn't seem so surprised but I was constantly disappointed. When I gave up chasing things it was a relief. There was something sweet and extraordinary about reality, even the grimmest reality. And there was something parasitical in the thought that there was always more to be had, either in another place, or with another person.

Lyuba first told me about Tanya and Vanya in letters sent from Moscow before she came to live in England. The letters arrived at my parents' house in Chalfont St Giles in blue envelopes, always two or three pages long so that the envelope had a nice weighty feel. They described her life in Moscow, her routine and her commitments, and sometimes they touched on her friends. She told me about Tanya, and of how Tanya talked about her love life with Vanya, and of how Tanya's explanations didn't shy away from even the smallest of details - though the letters didn't touch on the details themselves. In one of her letters she told of Vanya's affairs, which were many. Lyuba was shocked when Tanya told her about them, but couldn't find quite the right word to express her feeling in English, opting in the end for 'perverted'. It wasn't quite right, and she knew this, and left a little note in the margin with a question mark. She had wanted to express something horrible that might happen, regardless of whether you might like the person. And she didn't mean something like an accident that might happen to a particular person, but something that changed the love and the trust between two people, which seemed a very great thing to me.

Sometime after dropping us off at the sanatorium, Tanya and Vanya separated for good. Vanya continued living in the old wooden dacha outside Moscow, grew fat, and stopped looking after himself. Tanya married the banker she had been seeing for a while and became aloof. In later years she would communicate with us by email, unlike Vanya who didn't bother to keep in touch at all. It was always nice to see an email from her in the inbox. Lyuba showed them to me with regret and a touch of jealousy. Tanya always told of how good life was, of her pay rises, of her new flat, her new cars, and of the holidays she now took with her new man. There would be emails from Turkey and emails from Kamchatka. When we received emails from Kamchatka, Lyuba would frown and pucker her lips and intimate that such a holiday would be wonderful, that she had always wanted adventure, and that Kamchatka was one of the places she had always dreamed of visiting. She said that it wasn't even a question of visiting it, far away as it was. There was a suggestion that life wasn't lived enough, that there was too much sameness and not enough experiment.

The last time I saw Vanya there was something wrong with his legs. He couldn't walk well and the house had the sour, airless smell you get when people drink hard and don't wash much. His brother had moved in, and the two of them were mending cars for a living.

•••

I'm settled behind a lorry loaded down with stone chippings, counting the expansion joints on a raised section of new road. Every so often there are work gangs and bright yellow excavators and dumper trucks. I think: probably it will be better to meet with Inyutin. If I find Vanya it will end badly for sure, in tears or in a stupor of drunkenness. And there's something else too. I don't like the idea of coming close to his unhappiness, I don't want to catch it. If I call on Inyutin we will not cry or despair. Maybe there will be some griping, but not with self-pity. He has a simple view of life that consists in making the best of a situation. He reminds me of those heroes whose black bronze busts are venerated in a long line outside the Kremlin walls, a person who managed to carve out a place for himself against the odds. There are lots of stories of ordinary Russians who carved out a place for themselves in the new Russia while others fell by the roadside, and they all sound the same, and they all sound like Inyutin's story. It's as if his life had followed a script. He had to find everything out for himself, of course, but that too was part of the script.

Inyutin is Lyuba's oldest friend, and one of those who first came to visit us in England amongst the crowd of users and hangers-on. Now he moves between his flat in Moscow and his factory in Maksatikha, half way between Moscow and St Petersburg. He likes his flat even though it's miles from the centre and far from the nearest metro station. He doesn't care, as he goes everywhere by car. And he doesn't care that he spends so much time in the stupendous Moscow traffic jams. That's just how it is. He drives a big off-road vehicle with leather seats that have a massage option, doesn't smoke, doesn't drink spirits, eats healthy food and takes exercise, skiing along the trails near to his apartment in winter, and walking in summer. He has a problem with his back. I've told him it's because he drives too much and that he should move nearer to the centre where he will not need the car for every little trip. His flat is on the fourteenth floor and is huge. From the windows you can see the forest and fields that stretch into the farthest distance to the west of Moscow. His mother's family comes from one of those outlying villages that you see in miniature from his window, scattered amongst the big open spaces beyond the last of the tower blocks. He likes the country. He enjoys making jam and pickling mushrooms. He has even taken to ice fishing, an occupation he used to despise.

'Alcoholics - all of them!' he used to say. And what he meant was that those people (and his father was one of them) who went ice fishing had given up on ambition. To dress in greased-linen wool-lined overalls, to pull on valenki, to don mittens and a fur hat and trudge to the frozen lake or pond or river, to drill your hole and dangle your line bated with oiled dough pellets, to sit hunched over the little black opening on a camp stool, de-icing the line and peering into the dark eye of water for hours on end in order to catch minnows the size of a finger, unhook them and let them freeze into a curl (it would take about a minute), seemed to him the death of ambition, the last hopeless act of a defeated person.

I first met him in Lyuba's old Moscow tenement flat near to the zoo. It was warm, and from the open second floor window you could hear the heavy grind of trucks shifting gears as they accelerated away from the junction on Presnensky Val. We sat around the kitchen table waiting for his friend, Sasha, to turn up. Inyutin wore a tie because he had been told that an Englishman from London was coming to supper, and he wanted to make an impression. He had a bright smile and thick dark hair brushed back off his high forehead. He looked like the portrait of Diaghilev by Leon Bakst, the same upturned nose, high forehead, and mocking expression.

He had just completed some translation work with the Soviet hockey team on a tour around Finland and was already looking for ways to invest the dollars he had been paid in. I had been identified as a possible business partner, but that evening I turned him down without thinking twice. In the end he took his money to Korea and bought handbags and belts which he then sold off the back of a lorry in Moscow. After two years of this wheeling and dealing he made a small fortune.

I remember visiting his small flat in Moscow. A loaded shotgun was kept in an umbrella stand by the front door. There were dollars everywhere, on the floor, all over the table, slipping behind the sofa cushions. He spent his evenings counting money. During the day he sold his stock. Later he sold cash registers, and finally he invested all his capital in a disused textile factory which he converted into a plywood operation. The logs were barked and hot-soaked and then cut into papery sheets on a spinning device with blades like an enormous rotating razor. The press stood right in the middle of the work space, a machine as tall as a house, that Inyutin had imported from Italy. In the annex there was a swimming pool and sauna.

It was hard to believe how much one person could achieve in such a short period. Not that the factory wasn't without its own difficulties. It was relatively unprofitable at times, and there were always problems, either with drunkenness in the workforce, or with logging in the spring thaw when the forest tracks were deep in mud, or with the export market, or the volatile domestic market. There were problems with the plywood's quality, and with the machines and the way they always broke down. Many problems were associated with the constant outflow of money that was needed to keep the crumbling building in a workable condition. Then there were also the problems of competition and of increased transport costs because the factory was not near a railway. So it went on.

At a certain point Inyutin began depositing money abroad in Switzerland. He wanted an English education for his two daughters, and for a while he came to live in London. He rented a flat in Kensington, spending more on rent in one month than most people do in a year. At the same time he was surprisingly mean in certain things. His rented London flat was always cold. He never threw food away, even when it was stale, because he said it was perfectly good and to do so would be wasteful. Then he would invite us out for dinner and rack up a huge wine bill. I tried to tell him that it wasn't normal, that you didn't need to spend such sums. In the end I think I got through to him. He left off his obsession with expensive burgundies and began drinking supermarket wine. Then he stopped drinking altogether, and grew his hair long. He let it go wild as it turned grey, like Martha Argerich. Finally he tied it in a ponytail, and left London for good.

He was on the phone most days to Lyuba and perhaps I should have worried, but I never did. It always seemed that the problems, if they arrived, would come from my side, and that it was me who was the one not wholly to be trusted.

13

Vologda is behind me. I'm travelling west and the sun outlines the big clouds massed up ahead. It's the same road I took from Moscow a week ago, and the same new car though it no longer smells so new. I haven't covered much ground yet, not in the Russian scheme of things. Just a scratch, a small mark on the map. The huge expanses cast a shadow that distorts the sense of time. You can see far into the distance but it takes a long time to reach the place you can see, and the furthest fields and woods hardly seem to move at all.

At midday I pull up at one of the picnic places and walk a little way into the forest. A whitish lichen spreads everywhere, and the ground is soft with accumulations of dead pine needles. I find a place to lie down in the blueberry bushes, roll my jacket up under my head and close my eyes.

When I wake I'm still clutching the car keys in my pocket. Something is crawling under my shirt up my back, and for a moment I have no idea where I am. The sun cuts through tall branches. It's still high so it can't be so late. I turn on my side and look at the light slanting down the violet-tinged trunks. Strange dream! I was in an office, something like the employment offices you used to get in England, functional metal furniture upholstered in grey material, plastic tables, office chairs. An orange sofa against the wall. Putin was sitting behind the desk like any normal office worker, a kind of functionary ready to process the next case. I walked forwards and suddenly found myself kneeling in front of his swivel chair. He tilted his head downwards and offered his hand which I pressed to my lips in gratitude.

It's a vivid, not particularly pleasant recollection. It feels a wrong thing to have done, to have been carried away by such enthusiasm. I stand up and shake my shirt. Then I try to think what the dream might refer to. Maybe it had something to do with the peeling bumper sticker we saw on the last leg of the drive to Solovki: *'Obama Chmo'*. *Chmo* is difficult to translate into English. Lyuba tried to explain that it was a cross between loser and 'piece of shit', a worthless thing or person; a schmuck, or putz, perhaps. Yet none of the words in English sounded right. She explained what kind of person it referred to by reminding me of the old employment offices I once attended. So probably that was where the idea of an employment office came from. And maybe the television programme we watched at breakfast had sparked something too: Putin the noble, Putin the protector. But why was I bending down and pressing my lips to his hand?

It's very quiet. A woodpecker taps somewhere high in one of the tall trees, energetic and very fast between the taps, like a Morse-code machine stamping out its message. I think back on the dream again, imagining what it must be like to be summoned by Putin, to be drawn to him closely, to be chosen.

Nick is writing a book, something to do with Russia. We met up the last time I was in London and discussed it. He had an idea to write about certain diaries that have recently been uncovered. He's a journalist who for a long time reported on all things Russian, but has recently been banned from travelling to Russia because of his involvement in television programmes that have smeared Putin's name in England. A policy operative from Moscow has dredged around looking for people to ban, and now Nick can't make his living like he used to. Two years ago we challenged each other to write books about Russia in time to coincide with the hundred year anniversary of the revolution, and while he may not even need to come to Russia to write his book it seems to me that that is what I'm doing now. In my dream Putin bestowed his blessing on something that doesn't yet exist.

To dream of Putin must be quite normal, at least for a Russian person. I suppose I should be grateful I didn't dream I *was* Putin. My godmother in London, who I hardly ever saw, and who in the old days used to hobnob with many world leaders, used to say he was sexy. She was married to Charles Powell, Margaret Thatcher's private secretary, and her house in Bayswater was used as an informal meeting point where officials could take a break from the round of duties. She talked of Gorbachev who visited, and later of Berezovsky, the most flamboyant of the oligarchs, who took dinner with her. When she met Putin she said he had a special look in his eyes, that he was the sort of man one couldn't help wondering what it might be like to spend time with under the duvet.

Just nearby is a clearing and a bank with more blueberry bushes. I wander over and start picking, putting the berries straight into my mouth. They are few and small, not like the fat ones in Vashutino. As I pick, I think on the book that is not yet written, and of Nick who used to go backwards and forwards on assignment from his base in East Dulwich to various trouble spots in Russia, using his old contacts, promoting stories, following stories. His films were all to a greater or lesser degree critical of the state and of its interference in the lives of its people, at home and in what used to be termed the near-abroad, the lands that under the terms of empire have always fallen into the categories of 'general expansion' or 'imminent collapse'. He filmed in Chechnya and Belarus and Ukraine. In Chechnya he made a film about the traditions of bride kidnapping. Later he made films about Crimea and its annexation, and about Putin's hidden wealth. In the end it was the film that delved into Putin's secret wealth that led to his troubles.

Nick's stories of persecution and gangster-style politics were shared out amongst our group of friends, and for a moment they made our lives seem more interesting. Some of his more ambitious ideas never got off the ground because, when it came to Russia, the commissioning editors always wanted the same angle: Russia could only be a problem. On a scale of moral and ethical values it occupied a low place. It wasn't so much bothered by neatness and cleanliness, and it was full of men and women who stole money which they spent on off-road vehicles and apartments in Spain. There were thugs, and there was a sinister entity, the state, (something like a criminal version of our so-called 'establishment') which lied compulsively. In the background was the holy shrine of Russian culture, where a few notables meditated sorrowfully on the situation. Tolstoy, let's say. Or Chekhov. Sometimes they would pluck out somebody less mainstream in the English version of things, Pushkin or Lermontov, perhaps. They didn't want to see past this. Sometimes it seemed as if they couldn't see past it. To find wrong and expose injustice provoked a reaction, and that was what they were interested in.

I tramp back through the low bushes to the car. On the ring road around Yaroslavl a car flashes me, then another. I look out for the hidden police car waiting to clock drivers for speeding and pocket a payment, but see nothing. Then, ten minutes later, I get waved to the side at a police checkpoint. I'm asked for my license and car documents. Nearby there are other cars and other traffic police. One of the cars is being searched. Two policemen are rummaging through the open boot, though not very thoroughly by the look of it. My officer is wearing green army fatigues and a blue cap. He's heavy set, just the uncompromising sort that one is always warned of. He asks me to get out of the car, reads through the documents, and then hands them back and tells me that I should keep my headlights on during the day.

14

Beyond the roadblock where a road curls off the flyover, there is a sign for the town centre and the train station. I remember Yaroslavl from a long time back. We used to escape to Yaroslavl when we needed to get away from people. I once camped there in the grounds of a billiard club, during the days of Communism. It rained non-stop and in my bag I had two Brazilian-imported chickens, given to me by Olga. At that time it was a great gift, but I could find nowhere to cook them. Eventually I took a train to Rybinsk and caught a river boat back to Moscow. The boat was due to stop at Klin, the town where Tchaikovsky worked alone in a house set back from the road at the end of a long drive, far from the distractions of the city.

I had been given a cabin with a round window that looked over the Volga to a distant wooded bank. I hung up my damp clothes and then took out the chickens. Olga had wrapped them well, and when I opened the first bag the long-sealed-up smell knocked me back. Without thinking twice I opened the porthole as far as it would go and dropped both chickens out, one after the other.

The car radio is still broken, and the signs for Yaroslavl have come and gone. Cars overtake four or five at a time. Sometimes they come in longer lines of ten or more, and once they commit you must give way until they have passed through. Sometimes I follow behind a group of overtakers myself, or else I take a deep breath, stick my foot to the floor and go out on my own. If you don't do this then sooner or later you become stuck behind the slowest lorries, the old wheezing trucks which keep a little to the side and spue thick clouds of exhaust as they change down gears to tackle even the slightest of inclines.

It's past one in the morning when I reach the outskirts of Moscow. I promised Olga that I would check up on the flat and see the neighbour who keeps an eye on things when nobody's around.

I need to take a packet to one of Olga's friends too, a woman who lives on the other side of town whose husband has just died. Lyuba handed me the parcel at the last minute before she got on the train at Arkhangelsk, and when I took it she told me that I'd met the woman when I first came to Moscow, and that her husband had been a mathematician, a professor at Moscow University. I couldn't remember anything about either of them, but I said I would do it.

The satnav takes me off the motorway just after a blue-domed Church at the junction with the MKAD ringroad. For a while the route follows the river, and then crosses a bridge and a mass of train tracks. The closer I get to Energetichaskaya Street the more familiar the rows of dark tenements are. It's not so busy and I manage to find a space to park opposite the big front doors to Lyuba's block. The ochre-painted wall that runs along the footway near the prison hasn't changed, nor has the row of ground floor windows protected from the street with rusty, fan-patterned iron grilles.

I'm not sure what to expect. Olga's spare fob clicks the latch when I hold it against the metal plate, and the door gives way. Inside it's dim and musty. When I press the lift button there's a clunk and a slow heave of pulleys. The cramped cubicle has five rows of buttons, with numbers etched into the steel and filled with blue colour. Once I'm inside the apartment I feel for the familiar fat light switch, and the rooms immediately fill with memories, not of events but of particular objects.

I go to the kitchen to put the kettle on and sit for a moment on the chair by the big window, double framed with enough space between the frames to slide empty jars, scrunched up plastic bags, bags of pasta. The flat is dusty and uncared for. There are photographs everywhere. Photos of Lyuba when she was a small girl, of her grandparents, of Olga and Nikolai on camping holidays, a photo of Lyuba and me in Crimea standing by an urn with a rocky hill in the background.

Nikolai's big china cup with a gold leaf pattern running around the rim, sits on the table next to a darkly rusted silver sugar pot. I lift the cup to my nose, shake in some loose tea leaves, and pour the boiling water. The reddish brown colour seeps upwards, but the dark strength keeps low in the drift of leaves at the bottom. This was the way Lyuba first taught me to make tea. In those days we used to put a piece of lemon in, sometimes honey, but the tea was always black and always made with loose leaves. I began to dislike the thought of tea with milk, and of the fuss that was always made over its preparation in England: the teapot, the tea cosy, the warming of the pot, the tea strainer - all the teatime ritual with its sandwiches and its ceremony. I had begun a new Russian style of life and my English habits were all being dumped, together with my English ways of thinking about things.

Moscow felt free and easy in those days. The restrictions were part and parcel of life, everyone understood them, and this shared inconvenience kept everybody in the same place and counted for more than the actual freedoms denied.

On that first visit I didn't have a permit to travel outside Moscow, and wasn't sure if I would be given one because I hadn't registered myself at the police station when I arrived. Some people counselled bravery. Others caution. In the end I was given a plan to behave in public always as if I was a deaf-mute. This would solve all problems. No voice, no problem. It was a variation on Stalin's psychotic aphorism 'no man, no problem'. Later I discovered that it was the same ploy considered by Lenin when he was living under cover in Switzerland, hoping to return to Russia as triumphant leader of the seething revolutionary movement. His only refinement to the plan was 'to pretend to be Scandinavian'.

I was inclined to ignore restrictions. There was a sense that the country reached far in all directions. Russia reminded me of those medieval pictures that showed the world with its fields and castles, its lords, ladies, and peasants, its woods and boar and unicorn, its fishes and fruit all existing beneath the canopy of a heaven punctated by stars, and presided over by a human of medium worth wearing a crown or holding a key. The heavenly authority existed beyond the plane of the picture as something does which is beyond the confines of understanding. Below the star-studded heavenly canopy life continued. Lords and ladies galloped through the fields. Workers dug the soil, or held hogsheads upturned and got themselves drunk.

The tapestry of life ran its course and in the far beyond, outside the picture, was the end of the world. Perhaps there was something there, exquisite or unfriendly and alien, but it was no more important or relevant than the space beyond the edge of the page.

It's strange to see the same things after a long time away. This chair I'm sitting on doesn't seem to have moved since I first sat on it. That was almost thirty years ago. If I could write a poem it would be about all these objects which haven't changed. That fridge, this chair, this view from the window of the red-brick tenements, the long quiet street opposite where the milk shop used to be. Everything in relation to each other. But what about those things which have gone, or have been destroyed? Shouldn't they be included too?

As a young child I was presented with a birthday gift from the Russian shop in Holborn: a varnished ping-pong bat with a dangling wooden ball, and a round of articulated chickens who pecked over and over in rotating order at the same worn patch of yellow paint. Around this time I was also given a book called *The Crocodile Who Ate the Sun* by the children's author, Korney Chukovsky. The book made such an impression on me that I still remember it now, as if each page had been physically imprinted on my memory. The sun had gone, eaten by the crocodile, and all the animals in the wood were upset. It became dark, the magpies chattered in alarm, the baby rabbits were lost. Only the lobsters who lived in the swamp dared to go about their business as normal. At last two rams were sent as emissaries to go and wake up the brown bear. A tremendous climax followed, a classic drama of good versus evil, with the entire world at stake. The last page, the page which showed the bear being hugged for his good work, was something of an anti-climax. It felt boring. But afterwards when I tried to sleep I had nightmares. I woke up and they didn't go away. I saw the crocodile in the clouds which drifted across the weary London sky. Looking back I now realise that I was being pursued by the same phantom of terror which had inspired Chukovsky. It was as if I had woken up in the shadow of a great murderer, the same shadow cast by the terror that held all of Russia in its vice-grip.

My grandmother, who had looked with horror at the map over

my bed, took much of what her fellow Evangelical church-goers told her literally. She pictured the Soviet Union as being paved all over like one massive city without grass. When challenged on this point she backed down and explained that the paving of the country was a plan in progress, soon to be completed in all its terrible evilness. It was certainly a horrible idea, but what upset her most was the elimination of religion. In everyday life she saw the Devil's work everywhere. This was a universal problem, but there was always something that could be done about it. In England (where we lived) or in Wales (where she lived), there were always the green shoots of goodness pushing up and getting the better of him (the Devil, or 'Old Nick' as she called him). It was a continuous fight, the same fight that was evoked so stirringly in the hymn *Onward Christian Soldiers*. In Russia, the Christian soldiers had all been beaten up for the time being. It was a desert for religion, concreted from end to end, with sulphur seeping up through the cracks. In my grandmother's eyes it was a kind of hell on earth.

My father was in the opposite camp. He had been in Berlin in 1945 when it fell, a very young private who had declined the right to train as an officer. Back in England, following his demobilisation, he returned to finish his studies in Oxford. His tutor, C. S. Lewis, became ill and gave tutorials from his hospital bed. There he explained to my father about his conversion to Jesus, and how it had happened on board a double-decker bus. My father never talked about Berlin, but he did mention this session with the famous writer who had been puffy and red, and breathed with difficulty. It had made a bad impression, and along with many of his contemporaries he became a socialist in spirit and mistrustful of religion. For him, Russia was a country of peace and idealism, while the capitalist west was always stirring up hatred and war.

I thought I was different and could see people for what they were. My grandmother was energetic, emotional, and quite correct in her way. My father was also energetic, but with energy that was more of a nervous kind. He was correct too: socialism was fair and just, you could not deny that.

And then came a moment that marked a decisive shift in my

attitude. I had always rejected my grandmother's deepest beliefs, but now I began to have second thoughts about my father's convictions too. A new angle on Russia had settled into my thinking, and while at first I didn't like it, there was nothing I could do to ignore it, or to un-see it.

I was with my parents in the kitchen during one of those rare, peaceful moments that sometimes descended unexpectedly in our house. My mother, who took very little part in our round-the-table political discussions, pointed to a picture of the Politburo that was spread over the front page of *The Times*. It was 1978. Seven old men in fur hats and boots stood on the snow in a line, looking at the camera. Their faces did it. Coarse, grasping, ugly. My mother said: 'Look at them!'. My father squinted as he looked, even though he had his glasses on. There was no denying the impression, as if every sort of vice had been given the freedom to etch its own mark, to massage the various features, noses, eyebrows, frowns and grins, so that they might convey as closely as possible an image of squalor.

The thing which seems strange to me now is not so much that I remember the black and white picture so exactly, but that from a more or less grainy image surrounded by newsprint I felt I could, even at that age, see right through the grins and frowns, those efforts to appear charming, and into those seven men's calculated emptiness. I recognised something in them that was in me.

In this kitchen, when I think about that moment in the kitchen of my childhood, and the photograph of the Politbureau in *The Times* that was passed around, I remember I wanted my father to back down, and that I was pushy. He held the newspaper very close, so it almost hid his face. My mother stood by the table. I waited unkindly, in the middle of the room: three figures, as in a portrait group by David Hockney, together but at the same time alone and isolated, each one separated from the other.

15

I'm in a queue for train tickets, hoping for a place on the evening sleeper going south. An email has come in from Kheda, Nick's contact in Grozny. Over the years she has put him in touch with all kinds of people, and now he has suggested that I meet her if I can. A woman in a white plastic mac, with a tanned, lined face, and a small dog in her arms is at the window making arrangements that have to do with her niece. Every question she needs to answer makes her pause and frown and reconsider. She has large gold earrings, huge hoops which dangle forward and knock against the plastic screen whenever she bends over to listen better to what is being explained by the cashier. When it's my turn I ask for a single ticket to Astrakhan. I have never been to Astrakhan, nor to Grozny. Tacked onto the wall above the ticket office is a picture of Elbrus, the mountain that towers over the other peaks in the Caucasus like a double Mount Fuji. Alexander Herzen remembered this mountain towards the end of his life when he was living in London: depressed and lonely, he sat in a dark room in Primrose Hill and examined his past. He wrote fondly of his wife and of their innocent courtship, he also talked of a German tutor who left his position in the family house in Moscow in a flurry of recriminations and wounded pride. The tutor, who promised never to work for the Herzen family again after a dispute with Herzen's father, travelled alone to the spa town of Pyatigorsk where he hoped to sell a stock of perfume he carried with him in his travelling valise. Three weeks into the trip, still full of an indignation that his tenacious German soul would not let go easily, he made an excursion into the foothills of the Caucasus and there, in sight of the double peak of Elbrus, he fell and cut himself. Some blood from his not-very-serious wound smeared a rock and at that moment, as he smelt the cologne from one of the broken bottles he kept in his pocket, and saw the red mark made by his own blood as it trickled across the grey, weathered stone, he realised his rebellion was over, and that whatever it was he had started to fight for was lost. The following day he packed his bags and returned to Moscow.

There was a time when I thought I might write something about Herzen and of the many parallels that were to be found, even in this one inconclusive episode, to Nabokov's life and work. Nobody had done this as far as I was aware, and for a while I became quite excited at the prospect. Herzen wrote *My Past and Thoughts* while he was separated from his wife and going through the trauma of an exile unwilling to pursue claims relating to the seizure of his family's estates. Seventy years later the Nabokov family lands were appropriated by the Soviets, and Nabokov left to become another famous exile, first in England and then, during the first productive years of his writer's life, in Berlin. Humbert Humbert, the evasive, mottle-skinned, monster-lover of *Lolita*, had been a perfume salesman. In a later book, *Pnin*, Nabokov's hero, is always on the road, and suffers countless self-inflicted humiliations in the manner of Herzen's humble but touchy German tutor. In real life Nabokov was to pursue the phantom of escapism in the mountains himself but in a different form, in the pursuit of butterflies. And then there was the episode narrated in Nabokov's own memoir, *Speak Memory*, written while perfecting the process of preserving the genitalia of butterflies in alcohol and glycerol solutions, when he reveals the cruelty suffered by his own indentured German tutor, and the urge his young self felt to drop marbles on the tutor's head as it descended beneath him on the staircase of the family house in St Petersburg. The ideas were many, and were filed in a large red cabinet at home. The blood-red cabinet was like the cabinet of Dr Caligari, a place to put the Russian ideas that had not yet killed me. Now it seems to me that they were the first of many attempts at writing this book, the false starts that needed to be got through before I could know how to begin.

I have arranged to meet Kheda on my way to Crimea. There's no timetable that must be stuck to, but I've penciled an itinerary in my notebook as an organised Englishman from a novel by Jules Verne might. Back at the flat I slip the ticket into my passport, and collapse onto a divan in the living room under a Modigliani print, one of his sad girls, trying to imagine a world that wasn't full of people leaving for a better place, of climbing out of trouble, of falling into difficulties, of moving forward, or of going backwards - of trying to get someplace else. It wasn't possible.

I shut my eyes and imagine taking a walk as my father used to encourage me to do when I was small. He called it palming and said that it helped clear the mind. This time I close my eyes and remember the blue-painted metal door off the unmade street in Sudak. I stretch out and put my hands through a slot where there is a sliding lock which needs patience and a knack to slide open. I fumble around in my imagined world with its narrow-angled view, and then begin down an alley with doors that let onto holiday rooms. Our room, with the sagging mattress, is half way along on the right side. Lyuba is wearing hotpants and a tee shirt that shows her tummy. She wants to go to the market. Then we'll climb a hill and camp for a night. We leave on a road made of huge concrete slabs, past peeling stucco buildings that form three sides of a square, past benches, walnut trees, a broken drinking fountain, a bust of Lenin.

Out of town the dusty trees thin out, stray dogs wander on the verges. We find a way up, past a factory. The hill is steep and long, and at the top is a bare patch with short grass and stones and a place to light a fire. The sun is down but it's still hot, and I gather wood without clothes in this lonely place. Later on, when it gets dark, we lie down but it's too hot to sleep. Far down in the valley the sound of a disco comes and goes. Perhaps I would like to be there, and not on this lonely mountain top. I think that Lyuba might also want this, but I don't ask her. It seems almost like bad manners to suggest that we might need more than ourselves to be happy.

...

There was a time in my student days, after reading *The Path to Rome*, when, for a brief time, I became a fan of Hilaire Belloc. Now I think to myself: if he walked all that way just to take Mass, then I can go to the Black Sea to swim again. As long as I don't try to keep up with the pace of his jokes – of their delivery and frequency – I should be all right.

The train leaves Paveletsky vokzal at six this evening. I look through my bag. There isn't much in it: a change of clothes, a small towel, plimsolls, a map, a notebook, two sandwiches wrapped in a paper bag, a cucumber from Vashutino, and for something to read, Turgenev's *Sketches from a Hunter's Album* in the Penguin paperback edition given to me by my landlord in Swiss Cottage on my seventeenth birthday. It's a dog-eared, much-read copy, with wrinkles running up the spine and a telephone number scribbled on the inside cover – an old London number with an outdated prefix. On the cover is an illustration of a young nobleman in an open carriage pulled by four wild horses careering through the open countryside.

I have checked that everything is switched off, and taken my rubbish out to the bins by the play area in the courtyard. There are still two hours before I need to leave. I walk to the window and pull open the net curtain. Just there, to the left of the road that used to lead to the old milk shop, is Lefortovo jail. There is a wall and beyond the wall a yard, then some buildings. It looks forlorn in the way of prisons, as if nothing is happening.

This is the room I slept in when I used to visit Lyuba in the early days. Once, in the autumn of 1993, I woke to the thuggish stamp of soldiers running in the street, a sound of boots thudding altogether against the tarmac of the road. A lot of them. A drumming sound, heavy and unbroken, not marching but running. No voices. Perhaps the soldiers were on a routine exercise that time. Trouble was brewing in Moscow and a curfew after dark had been announced. I can picture a phalanx of young men with shaved heads and jack boots turning the corner at the top of the street. But what I remember more vividly is the absence of people and the pale beginnings of morning light catching the tall red-brick tenements all the way down to the junction at Aviamotornaya.

The following night I walked the deserted streets until I reached the centre, where the fighting was. There were blockades on Gorky street, piles of furniture, wheelie bins, planks of wood, steel girders, and rocks and rubbish of all kinds heaped across the road. What was this improvised barricade there to stop? Tanks? But whose tanks? It was a people's blockade, and there were fires in the side streets. The people's militia gathered in a comradely fashion. Cigarettes were passed around. I was taken for a foreign journalist and treated kindly. I wanted to see some action. These fires on Gorky Street were fine, the camaraderie was fine, as were the huge piles of rubbish deposited across the wide streets in a gesture of tank-defiance. But where were the tanks, and where were the soldiers?

I asked and was told: 'Down there!' A man dressed in a leather coat gestured. I looked down the line of buildings and at that moment heard the sound of automatic gunfire. It was a block away, maybe two. The shots were whip-like, and quickly swallowed in the cool night air. They sounded out of place, almost childish, as if a silly game was being acted out by losers.

I run through images of these disturbances, this end-of-an-era time, on a computer set up on a circular table covered in magazines. Now these moments have gone down in history their meaning looks clear and understandable. A story emerges with men that don't seem to be directing events but reacting to them.

There are pictures of Gorbachev, pictures of tanks, of Red Square, and of the smoke-blackened parliament building. There are pictures of Yeltsin, and of crowds swarming in the streets. There's a picture of Gorbachev with a young, fleshy Putin.

Gorbachev always comes across in the same soft-edged way, a man who can be counted on not to upset anyone. There's a photo of him bending over on a road somewhere in Siberia, holding his ever-welcoming hand out to a squirrel. Another picture links back to an archive of younger Gorbachevs: Gorbachev with his young wife, Raisa, Gorbachev with his grandparents on their farm in Stravrapol, Gorbachev as a fresh-faced law student in Moscow State University.

Pictures of the failed coup d'état in 1991, during the last days of August, are less dramatic. It had been wet in Moscow, and for days the sky stayed dark and heavy with more rain. The first action was taken by a special army team dispatched to arrest Gorbachev in his holiday dacha by the sea in Crimea, and cut off his communications. Once this operation was complete a message was broadcast on television and radio explaining how the acting government would step in to handle the crisis, how they needed to take over in order to save the Union from collapse, and how Gorbachev was sick due to his workload. They talked about continuity. In the meantime, in a private session down at the dacha in Crimea, they asked Gorbachev to sign his resignation. He refused. The plotters then ordered tanks to the parliament building, declared a state of emergency, shut down all scheduled programmes on television and broadcast a performance of Swan Lake.

But they didn't go about their job as efficiently as they might have. They hadn't arrested Yeltsin who had seen the extremely suspicious Swan Lake performance on the television in his own dacha just outside Moscow. Immediately he began phoning his own people. The tide of public opinion was with him, and for all the new freedoms. The ballet broadcast was enough to freeze the blood in everybody's veins. People expected a barrel of lies very soon, because that was what this beautiful classical dance meant: something dangerous is on the way and you, the people, should get yourself prepared. It had happened before, and it was happening again.

Yeltsin asked journalists to write something and then photocopied their words and distributed them to the crowds before it was too late. 'We must not let these monsters win this time! Defy them!' it proclaimed. Yeltsin marched with his supporters to the parliament building where the tanks had already arrived. There he put one foot on the heavy tracks and climbed up to deliver his plea by megaphone.

Meanwhile the plotters made the mistake of holding their own press conference. They all look incredibly seedy, and three days later they were arrested. The army, which had been waiting to see which way the wind blew, came down on the side of liberty against repression. Liberty was where the big bucks were. Repression was a mug's game - for the moment - and the coup fell away to nothing.

The final picture in this sequence shows Gorbachev's return. He steps out of the plane at Sheremetyevo still in his holiday gear, wearing a white zip-up coat and soft white trousers. He looks exhausted and weak, and grips onto the handrail as if surprised to find it's still there. His political life was finished though he didn't yet realise this. He began to work up his position once more, but this time it didn't make any sense. He was caught between two impossible-to-reconcile forces, the forces of continuity responsible for the failed coup, and the forces of change led by Yeltsin.

Gorbachev had become a nobody, in the middle. He dreamed of a socialist state, and of a continuation of the old union of republics, but based his leadership on a stand against all the forms of violence and repression that had always kept the socialist union together. When he arrived back from his arrest in Crimea he began where he had left off, as if nothing had happened. There were appeals to reform the party, even though its incompetent and vicious face had just been shown on television sets across the world. To preserve the idea of the Soviet Union he found himself having to defend something rotten and indefensible.

His impossible position became a public matter and on the 24th August 1991 he dissolved the Central Committee of the Communist Party. Exactly four months later, on Christmas Day, he resigned.

A break-down of economic control followed. A few people rode high on the un-regulated sales of state-owned property, while at the same time I remember how half of Moscow was on the street selling whatever they could lay their hands on. The finance minister had announced freedom to buy and sell anything, anytime, and almost overnight the city turned into a bring-and-buy sale. On every corner and at every subway entrance ordinary people waited with items in their open hands, or placed on blankets on the ground: the contents of a kitchen drawer, a cucumber, a camera, some buttons.

I scroll down to a picture of the parliament building, the so-called White House, all blackened and burnt. This was taken in October 1993, when a second, more vicious uprising was attempted. Many people died on the streets and at the television centre, and at the parliament building where the old party leaders were holed up. The hospitals were full with the injured.

In this chaos I can pin down my movements twenty five years ago to the day, and to the hour. The shots I heard were rounds being discharged on Nikitsky Street. It was the night before Yeltsin's order to fire on the parliament building, and the following morning I watched as the tank took aim at the White House on television. There was a puff of smoke and a few seconds later the sonic boom shook the windows in this living room where I'm sitting now.

And so it was all over for a second time. The plotters were led out of the building in front of the television cameras, looking even more wretched than the original lineup two years previously. It was sunny with a cool wind. Small, ragged clouds, low in the sky persisted in their pinkish brown colour all through the day. I walked the streets again. It felt like winter was on its way. There were bullet holes in the trolleybuses and in the thick plate glass of the 1905 Street metro station, just up from the zoo. I found myself going over lines from Wordsworth that I had been forced to learn for my final school examinations: *'Our birth is but a sleeping and a forgetting...'* and: *'Heaven lies about us in our infancy!/ Shades of the prison-house begin to close/ Upon the growing Boy'*

There was a part missing, but I could remember: *'The youth, who daily farther from the east/ Must travel, still is Nature's priest,/ And by the vision splendid/ Is on his way attended;/ At length the Man perceives it die away,/ And fade into the light of common day'.*

It was the line: *'And fade into the light of common day.'* that did it for me. Those clouds that drifted across the pale sky that day were neither dark nor light, but slightly brownish. They glowed very faintly with the light of a common winter day and were on their way to dimness and darkness. Probably they were not the sort of clouds Wordsworth had in mind. He made his poem an analogy of the progress of a day, from morning through to the midday, from youth to maturity. This was a little different. It was an intimation of winter, a seasonal progress. The poem had been comparing a man's life with a single day. During this period in Soviet history, two or maybe three generations of idealism were washed away, some people said in a matter of hours, others said months. By the time Yeltsin took control it had gone for good.

It's strange now that there are no people in this flat. It was so often the scene of crowds of people, all gathered to talk and drink. I had arrived in a country I didn't know, into a family that had not yet become mine, and I saw for the first time something wholly different, in effect a continuous revolution. Here were people who often celebrated socially, whose social intercourse was dissident and active. I had grown up in a different world, somewhere settled and finished, a place where people slotted inevitably into a position in society, high or low. In Chalfont St Giles and in Chorleywood, everything worked like clockwork and everybody knew their place. Everybody had a job, or else they didn't have one and you knew about it. They were the sort of person who couldn't get one, or else they didn't need one and had independent means. In Moscow, at that time, it was different. Those people who visited were all of the same hard-to-pin-down type. They may have had jobs or made money, but it didn't seem to matter much. Their work was not so relevant. The real dramas took place at home, in unending cycles of discussion and argument.

Arriving in this flat with all its associations was an introduction to Soviet dissident life at a time when that life was almost finished. Those people who used to visit were the last of a type that suddenly became extinct. It was as if a big axe had been hanging over all of them, ready to fall. And then it did fall, and the conversations and arguments became irrelevant. That happened practically overnight when there was nothing more to laugh about, when the old Socialist ideals were officially written out of history, and people, even those who had considered themselves to be above the fray, couldn't bear to watch as everything flowed away.

Olga's cousin, Zinik, left Russia much earlier, during the seventies, when the English had yet to form the oligarch image and perceived Russians abroad, first and foremost, as bearded, jumper-wearing dissidents. Zinik, who had always been clean-shaven, arrived first in Israel and then in London, where he stayed and became a kind of honorary citizen of Soho, re-working his own emigration story into his novels and short stories. He returned to Russia for the first time just as it was toppling on the edge. The conversations had changed, and there was no interest in the state of the country any more, of how it had got to where it was, or what direction it should take next. Now the talk was all of publishing deals, of television deals, of opportunities to be grabbed. The tsunami of Russian immigration to London appalled him at first. He felt that his own London, the London of his emigrant dream, beautiful and unique, was being trampled on by a herd of ignorant farm hands with crew-cuts, all dressed in the same tracksuits and white trainers.

Leonid, Olga's brother who co-ran a publishing house in Moscow when I first turned up, was living in this same flat, and I remember him in the morning, tramping around the always-warm rooms in red running shorts, a cotton shirt and sandals, making himself strong coffee and preparing for the day ahead. Sometimes I drove for him, acting as a chauffeur in a little red Zhiguli.

There was a recklessness in the air and an acceptance of all mistakes. I'm the same age as Leonid was then, and I feel it. My position has shifted. It's as if I've been given a second go, another chance to piece it all together. Back then I was travelling through Russia with my eyes wide open to what was new. Now I'm looking at it from the outside in. I can see my own mistakes, and at the same time I see mistakes everywhere in others. There is an ever-growing anxiety that turns quickly into outrage. A carnival message of good hope, bad taste, idealism, and even of paranoia, is held up for serious scrutiny by truth-seekers. Out of the natural chaos of life, people hang on to a single message and cry out with righteous passion as if they were drowning. The story of Russia has become narrow and straight, like an easily solvable riddle. Everything is taken too seriously, too literally. If there was a way to loosen things up, to push wider the opening that has become so choked with the same tired phrases, the same old words.

Nothing has changed, but everybody has gone. The photographs are all that is left of those people who lived here and came to visit, old ones set in elegant frames propped up on the furniture, or big blow-ups without frames tacked to the walls, tiny black and white ones with thin borders, and colour ones from recent times. A lot of faces which make a big impression of sadness, as if you could see each life flashing past, each life caught in one instant without a future.

I'm not sure if Olga and Nikolai will come back to this flat. Olga has talked about emigrating to Israel, and if she does Nikolai will follow. Perhaps they will go there for his treatment, and if they do then the flat will be rented or sold, all the things in it will be boxed up and moved, and there will be nothing left except the view from the windows and perhaps the smell in the corridor.

I lock the door and wait for a moment, listening. The building feels like a relic, something from another era that has been forgotten about. The green colour of the walls has not changed, nor has the stale smell. The partition which I helped to build with Nikolai all those years ago is still standing. He wanted to build it to make the corridor to the last three flats more private, and we went to the forest together in January to get wood for the studding. I suppose the trip might have been encouraged by Olga as a way to bond after the difficult times we had had in the early days, when I was new on the scene and my presence was bound up with the break-up of Lyuba's first marriage. Nikolai tucked a small axe into his belt and we set off in our felt boots and fur hats. We took the train to a small stop just out of town where the forest was deep with snow, and the fallen trees, and half-fallen trees crossed each other in a tangled pattern of uprights and diagonals. And then we returned with three pieces of freshly cut timber to the quiet station platform, that had been swept so you could see the cracked yellow tiles beneath a layer of grey ice.

16

The light is already fading when I arrive at Paveletsky vokzal. It could be a French station but at the same time it's pure Russian; a barrack building with slated roofs, dormer windows, and detailed stonework to either side of the central entrance. Inside it's portioned up like an exhibition hall, and on the first floor there's a high-ceilinged waiting room with rows of chairs all facing a big timetable on the wall.

An old man slouches awkwardly on the hard seats, with a circle of bags on the floor around him. Near him is a rough-looking group, already far gone with drink. One of the men keeps turning his head suddenly and challengingly from his sitting down position as if he had seen something important on the other side of the hall by the restaurant buffet. Another stands stiffly in a pork-pie hat with his hands in his pockets and his body awkwardly hunched, like a golfer preparing to putt. They all have the same tanned, dirty-looking necks and wrists. I settle myself down in the middle of the central stand of seats near to a young family, mother, father, and two silent children, who wait beside an enormous blue suitcase.

I put my bag on my knees and stare at the timetable: Kursk, Ryazan, Samara, Ufa, Astrakhan. The last time I was in Crimea I was a young man chasing a young woman. Now my body aches in the morning and I pray the future will be kind to me. I have childish hopes to find something that was lost a long time ago, and a planned-out route on my phone which I've sketched into my notepad. It runs as far as the the patchy area of marsh around the Caspian Sea - the blue tongue on my old map - before diverting through the mountains to Chechnya, and then onwards in a westerly direction to the Black Sea.

At just before midnight the train begins to move. I have spent extra on a seat that will serve as a bed. Somebody has already taken the bunk above mine and settled down for the night. A woman and her grown-up daughter sit opposite me. Standing at the open door is a young man with folded arms wearing a yellow jumper. He looks hard, maybe a little dangerous. A girl rushes up to him from the corridor, whispers instructions, and then darts off. He keeps his eye on the empty bunk. My bag is stowed safely and I could go to sleep, but I'm not tired and the kid standing at the door bothers me. I would like him gone but the guard looking after the carriage seems to have an arrangement with him, letting him stay where he is when she walks past delivering bedding. The woman and her daughter leave for a short while, then reappear in tracksuits.

The daughter wishes me a good night and returns to the next compartment. Her mother settles down until she is completely hidden beneath a pile of blankets. The lights are dimmed, and while the yellow-jumpered man still leans suspiciously against the open door, I get myself comfortable with my head next to the window and my phone in my pocket, while the suburbs of Moscow run away behind us.

17

It's four in the morning. The man in the yellow jumper is on the top bunk, curled up and facing the wall without bedding. There is a steady muted roar from the train which is running at full speed. When I press my face to the cool glass I can make out trees, bushes, fields. We pass through a level crossing with a signal box, then the familiar outline of trees begins again, everything moving past very quickly and without let up.

I can't sleep, and I don't want to read. I take out my phone and wait for the map to load. Empty green and grey areas show to either side of a thin black line. At five o'clock the line divides, and the blue locator dot starts to wind upwards towards Tambov.

I remember Tambov from years ago, and the impression of misery and poverty at the railway station. That was in 1993 when I was on my way south to help Nikolai with the bee farm he ran with his Moscow friends every summer. A week later, in a broken-down village near to Borisoglebsk, I was dragged out of bed by Olga's brother, Leonid, who had driven all through the night to pick us up.

'You're lying like pigs in the country while Moscow burns!' he said.

I sat on the edge of an old iron bed in my pants, rubbing my eyes, still half asleep. Nikolai packed some bags. There was no telephone in the village. No mobile phones. No way to communicate in a hurry.

Now I wonder if I am making the same mistake – travelling in the opposite direction, away from the action, but this time even further. Important orders always come from one place. In Russia they come from that irregular purple blob, the centre of the web that used to stretch across the whole of the Soviet Union. Two years ago it seemed the dark centre had begun to pulse madly, even though preparations had been underway for a long time. Old plans, resolutions, and declarations were laid over impulses that traced the fate of Crimea right back through history. And now everything has been jumbled up again, and everybody is at loggerheads, everybody wants to kill each other, everybody wants to prove they are right.

I look out of the window at the dark outlines of trees. If I look hard enough I can make out the repeated diving and rising-up pattern of the overhead cables following the train on the edge of the track. A man sidles up the corridor, looks into our compartment, and is gone again. I unwrap a honey sandwich from my bag and take a bite.

Light begins to seep upwards from the horizon at a little before six o'clock. By seven the woman hidden by blankets has washed and changed, and is sitting in the corner sipping tea with her daughter. My steaming black tea, brought to me by the guard, is standing on the table next to my second sandwich, this one with ham pushing out. I alternate bites of the sandwich, with cold bites of the stubby cucumber grown in Vashutino.

The train stops at Michurinsk for a long while, and then at Tambov for a few minutes, just long enough to stretch my legs while keeping an eye on any signal from the carriage guards who stand near to their open doors in a long line down the platform.

And then we are off again, this time heading south east for Saratov. We pass through miles of empty country with here and there a village, or a river, or a church with a cluster of domes standing alone on the top of a hill as if watching over a land of innocence and dreams. Now there is only the mother and her daughter and myself in the carriage, and there's plenty of space to spread our bags around. Natalya tells me that she's been looking for a job, so far without success. Her mother listens and nods whenever I look across at her. The girl is sweet and optimistic. She's pretty and healthy looking, and believes that one day she really will get a job in Moscow. And yet there are so many applicants for each job – everybody wants to work in Moscow. All the girls look nice, do their hair, dress up, study. The mother has seen it all before and looks downcast.

'Where are you travelling to?' Natalya asks.

'I have a ticket to Astrakhan. Afterwards I'll go to the mountains, to the Caucasus.'

'Will you climb?'

'Maybe, if I get that far, but I'm not a climber.'

'Don't forget the market!' Her mother puts in.

'What kind of market is that?' I ask.

There's a silence, and then Natalya begins again. 'The fish market in Astrakhan! It sells everything. Anything you could want. It's famous all over the world. They have huge sturgeon! And caviar. The best caviar in Russia! It's amazing, beautiful! You must go!'

As she talks she gestures with her hands to describe the size of fish that are for sale. Her mother's eyes light up in agreement and she nods her head and begins smoothing the folds of her dress across her lap.

We have exhausted ourselves for the moment. Natalya's mother takes out a book of Sudoku puzzles and two pencils. Soon they are both engrossed in a problem.

I flick through my Turgenev. Nature crowds the pages. Leaves flutter. Shadows filter through the forest. A big sun rises. The moon slips out of a high cloud. Rooks scream as they wheel over a ploughed field. Mist settles on a marsh. Drops of blood stain the ground next to the limp bodies of dead birds.

The carriage sways very slightly to the rhythm of the track. I look across at Natalya. She raises her knee and puts a foot on the seat, clasping one hand round her ankle. She looks so desirable that I have to press my forehead to the window and concentrate on the moving landscape to change the direction of my thoughts. And perhaps, after all, it's all in my head anyway. To anybody entering the carriage the mother and daughter look simply stuck, heads down, limbs static, frozen in attitudes of failure as the endless beauty of Russia flows past outside. They form the perfect picture of homework-malaise, a still life of mental immolation. Traces of boredom show in Natalya's face, the mother is less bothered – less bothered about finding a solution and less bothered about failing to find a solution.

Natalya passes me the puzzle and explains what needs doing.

They have six hours to finish it before their stop at Pallasovka, just near to the border with Kazakhstan. Six hours is a long time and I don't want to have them sitting around staring at me, so I copy the boxes and numbers out in my notebook, using the squared paper as a grid. Before I have time to finish, the beautiful pastoral landscape falls away and we draw into Saratov. Natalya and her mother are staying put, but I need to stretch my legs again. It's the last-but-one stop before Astrakhan, which we are due to reach early in the morning.

I buy a litre of water and a packet of biscuits from a vendor set up outside the station entrance, and take a stroll across the square. The open space is bathed in soft orange light. A group of young men with Asiatic faces are being questioned by two policemen under an enormous statue of Dzerzhinsky. They stand by their bags looking small and uncomfortable. A little further from the station I hear the sound of an excited crowd. It's a football stadium and the nearer I get the more distinct the sounds become. There's a constant feverish baying that turns from time to time into a continuous roar, like the final crash of a wave. One of the teams is on the attack. You can sense the rhythm of the game, the way one side breaks away and comes close to goal. It's clear that a large section of the crowd believes they will soon score, but the final eruption of sound, the 'full stop' of an actual goal that would signal the end of all other sounds is not forthcoming. It feels wild and raw.

When I arrive back, Natalya and her mother have changed out of their tracksuits and have their bags ready in the overhead racks. The mother has a serious, distant look, as if she had already begun to think of home. Natalya has changed too, and is less inclined to talk. The train is almost empty. Soon after leaving the station we begin to follow the course of the Volga on its western bank. There are cranes, docks, everything fading off into the hazy distance. For a while the train runs high on an escarpment and then the river is gone, snaking off to the east again. Nearby is the famous car plant that was built in collaboration with Fiat, birthplace of the ubiquitous Lada, and the place where Berezovsky, the oligarch who groomed Roman Abramovich and visited my godmother in London, made his first fortune.

There's a different guard looking after our carriage. She looks Kazak with her high cheekbones and dark eyes, or maybe Mongolian. Before Pallasovka, Natalya and her mother give up on their problem solving. They want me to have their book as a going-away present, and I tell them that I will copy more of the puzzles into my notebook instead.

It's nearly dark when they wish me goodbye. They tell me that the train will pass by a massive salt lake, quite dry, and that for a moment I will be in Kazakhstan because of the way the map is drawn.

'But it's only for a short while,' Natalya looks at me and smiles. 'Then you will be back in Russia again,'

'That's good,' I reply.

Natalya is already on the platform. Her mother backs out of the compartment door and starts shuffling down the carriage.

I'm on my own again. Soon we will reach the steppe, the flat lands which continue onwards and eastwards into the huge territory of Kazakhstan, the empty places that are almost uninhabited except for those small creatures that burrow in the sand. Places of purity, testing grounds for rockets, testing grounds for nuclear bombs, old military zones, closed areas with launch pads, places full of secrecy and nothingness.

The train has a different feel now that it's running nearly empty. In the corridor the last remaining passengers, including one newly-boisterous man who introduces himself as an employee of Gazprom, have shed a layer of formality. The few people still left in the compartments stare back with the same challenging look. They slouch in their seats now they have the space to themselves. They talk loudly, and there is an edge to their conversation and to their reactions, especially to their laughter, that wasn't there before. Even the train itself has changed. The clattering of the wheels has become louder, and the doors to the smoking area between the carriages slam more violently. It's already dark, and in my compartment there's nothing to do but pull my blanket up and gradually fall to thinking as we pass through the emptiness.

I try to rid myself of the image of Russia as it might appear on the front cover of a catchy book, a place of backward letters, red sickles, and bottles of vodka. In the salons of Paris during the 1880's there was talk of the latest Russian novel to hit the bookshelves and of its passion and devil-may-care characters, and of how incredibly 'Russian' it all was. The same undercurrent of understanding is disturbed now when people hear of intrigue and extravagance, of the casual flouting of accepted rules of behaviour, and the murder of undesirables.

Lyuba complained when Olga gave an old china clock to Zinik's sister, Tata. Tata was unreliable, she drank, she had many lovers. Her lifestyle was not censured in any way, but it was known of and talked of, and Lyuba said that the clock which had been brought back from the ruins of Berlin after the war's end by her grandfather - the same clock that had stood on her mantelpiece since she could remember - would simply disappear. Lyuba talked of the beautiful china clock, of its white face and of the gold cherubs clambering up its sides, and of the cherub's rosy puckered lips, as if it had been a part of the family.

I tried to calm things down. 'You can't blame your mother,' I said. 'And besides, we owe Tata after she was so kind to us'. Then I reminded her of the time we met Tata on the station platform. 'You remember how she was so welcoming and gave us the key to her house?'

This was all true. Tata met us at the station with a key in her hand, large and energetic in a dissolute way. I think she liked the idea of trouble and of scandal that involved people jumping into bed with each other, and she probably knew that I wasn't quite approved of. She gave me a hug and, even covered up as she was, in furs, I could sense the unmistakable warm carelessness of a person who had never made a habit of worrying too much about preliminaries.

We thanked her and left for Galich. There was snow everywhere. I remember the old mining town and the provincial station, its waiting room hung with a huge canvas of Lenin leading the people. Lenin wore a flat cap and held a red flag tilted forwards, just as his own body leant forwards. Somewhere beyond the edge of the smoke-darkened scene lay the future, glowing with dull, apocalyptic light.

I was reading a lot in those days, trying to catch up, or rather to join up those things I already knew to make a more coherent picture. I wanted to grasp everything, and the more I read the more the gaps opened up. I had come under the spell of Leopardi and his great pessimism. That the entire population of the world, except for Leopardi and a couple of his friends from student days, acted at all times with cynical self-interest didn't strike me as odd in the least. I wanted to learn, and to learn you had, at first, to believe. Reflection came later. It might take years to have second thoughts. And then there were the third thoughts. There was plenty of time.

Galich station was messy with swept snow and once we left the platform the town was immediately quiet, though you could sense life inside the houses. Old nineteenth-century rows of merchants' houses with odd blank windows and lines of broken cornicing gave way to blue or green painted wood houses with ornate fretwork and dilapidated first floor conservatories, then to smaller dark-wood houses, and workshops and yards. Piles of coal were dumped on street corners. White smoke trailed upwards from iron flues and brick chimneys, and there was a sulphurous smell to the cold air that felt good.

It was still early in the day and we had time to buy supplies from one of the food shops designed in the old days to a unified plan, the modular constructs that had all been built in the same way, and were now all falling apart in the same way, with the same chipped and cracked tiles, the same broken entrance steps where the partially exposed iron reinforcing bars had been worn thin to a dull pewter with the rub of feet. We found a bread shop, and bought two bottles of vodka at a kiosk for presents.

At midday we caught a bus at the station square, and half an hour later were dropped off at the edge of a forest. We walked for two hours on a wide path cleared between the drifts. There were no vehicles, though you could see the track marks of earth-moving equipment. On the first long incline I began to measure our progress by counting telegraph poles, one every seventy metres, but that got boring. The inhuman scale of the landscape crushed the spirit. Then we reached a level place, and I realised that my spirit had not been crushed by the inhuman scale of the landscape but by the hill, and everything became more pleasant. In places the sun cut through the trees, and the snow burned brightly as if a tin sheet had been laid flat on the ground. Blue shadow filled the forest, and in the drifts near to us the same blue shadow glowed even more intensely. Many of the trees were fallen. Sometimes a flurry of snow would cascade through the branches and land with a dull thump on the ground. There were magpies (soroki). If there was just one soroka I would greet it, and touch my forehead.

I wondered whether Napoleon had ever read Leopardi. I asked Lyuba: 'What do you think? Do you think he might have read him?' She didn't like to be asked something she wasn't sure how to answer, and kept quiet. I continued my train of thought as we trudged on in silence. Perhaps, just before he died, he might have got hold of a first copy and felt a pang. On the other hand this was unlikely. I decided that the endless white road in front of us must have been very much like the endless white road taken by the Grand Armée with its hundreds of thousands of foot soldiers, its gun carriages and supply carriages, its officers on horse, its field hospitals, and its prisoners. Once on its way to Moscow and then, having found nothing solid to conquer, on its way back again to Paris. By then the army was ragged and worn-out, and still full of conscripts, including the Italian conscripts mourned by Leopardi who were dying, not by iron, but by clouds and wind for the same Frenchmen who had murdered Italy.

The village was deserted, but we found a house where people lived who knew to expect us. In the failing light they took us to the last house at the edge of the forest, opened it up, and showed us how to light the fire and where to get water. We lit the old stove with its bed-above, and then returned to let them know that everything was okay. There was already a big bowl of soup set in the middle of the table. A nice-looking blond boy of around fourteen began to eat. Then his father dipped in with his spoon. When the grandmother and grandfather joined in, I understood that we weren't going to get bowls for ourselves but that we should all eat from the one big bowl. Tumbler-size glasses of vodka were filled for everybody. I watched as the fourteen year old sagged. His eyes shone and, with a piece of bread still in his hand, he began to stare at Lyuba, his lips swollen, saliva gathering at the corners of his mouth.

Later that night we returned to our house and climbed in to the bed on top of the stove, just as they used to do in the old Russian fairy stories. The village people said this was dangerous, that noxious fumes from stoves that hadn't been lit for a while could lead to death. Outside it was forty below. We lay on our high-level bed close to the ceiling, cuddling up to keep warm. I began to think of the snow outside, of the young boy who had been so quickly affected by the vodka, and by the sight of a beautiful woman sitting at his table. Then I thought of how I would have to break the ice in the morning to get water from the pond, about the tall piles of frozen shit I had seen earlier in the outhouse - an unsettling sight that brought to mind cataclysmic cold of a type that could not be imagined in England. I wondered about the absence of any communication back to Moscow, and of the likelihood of being found dead, asphyxiated by noxious fumes from the long-unlit stove. Suddenly there was a knock on the door.

'Lyuba! Ah, Lyuba!'

It was Alyosha, the father of the boy. He had been quiet at the dinner table but now he was drunk.

'We're going to Galich...Lyuba!'

It was dark in the house, and where we lay above the stove I couldn't see my hand in front of my face. Aloysha's deep, coaxing voice, called from the doorway.

'Ah Lyuba, Lyu...We're going...'

He must have drunk a whole lot after we left, and was letting go of the feelings that had gathered inside him so strongly and quickly, without any restraint. I was an Englishman and therefore of not much consequence. He was Russian and now he wanted this beautiful Russian woman who lay next to me.

'Lyuba!'

He stumbled forward and banged against the cupboard. Perhaps he could hear us breathing.

'We'll see the drivers! There'll be a party...' He swore quietly, and then began talking in a mumble.

The following morning I checked the thermometer on the table. The stove had done its job, and the mercury showed a comfortable fourteen degrees. I stoked the fire at the front where the big opening for logs was, and then opened the hot-air pipe at the back. Lyuba was still curled up under the pile of blankets. We had survived the night, and now had to get water, chop wood, and cook for ourselves.

The Leopardi was open on the table at that point in his long poem dedicated to the humble broom flower, when the tremendous question of God and of the Son of Man who had come to save Man was raised, the moment when he asks how it is that we presume it to have been so, how we could have ever decided that we were due to be saved, that we merited saving.

...

Beyond the reflection in the carriage window there's nothing to see: it's all black and the rattle of the wheels falls away quickly. My sheet and extra blanket are still in the plastic bag, on the empty seat opposite me. I have opened the contents of my wallet on the table, counted out the money bills, and put half back into my wallet and half into my passport with my ticket.

Before we left Vashutino, Nikolai talked of a salt lake, the same one that Natalya mentioned before she got off the train with her mother. Apparently it was a wilderness as impressive as the salt desert in Utah, and according to the map on my phone the train must have been passing it now, all dried up and white in the dark. Nikolai used to work nearby in the military zones where rocket systems were tested. Nick talked of this place, too, and of the contamination from the fallout of hundreds of tests that took place over the years. It was here, in the top secret prison camp and research facility known as The Installation, that the first Soviet hydrogen bomb was exploded, and where Andrei Sakharov, the most famous of the bomb's developers, began his long dissident journey.

A witness in one of Svetlana Alexievich's books talks of Karaganda, which was at that time just one of many labour camps built right in the middle of the empty steppe lands. Surrounded at all times by guards with dogs, and petrified of the outside world, she would watch her mother, along with the other mothers, leave for work through the barbed wire. Later on, when she was five, she was removed to an orphanage and taught that her mother was bad, that she had been an enemy, and that Stalin was wonderful. When she returned thirty years later to see the remains of the camp during Gorbachev's Perestroika, she wished she hadn't. She finally tracked down a very old and penniless woman, the same one who had taught her to hate her mother. In a restaurant she overheard the drunken conversation of men who still stuck up for everything. Her own parents were long dead, and all the suffering turned out to have been in vain; there was nothing of any value left that she could see in this world.

18

I wake to the sound of cleaning. The sun is up, trees and fields speed past the window – no steppe anymore. My compartment door is open, and the guard with the dark hair and high cheekbones has taken off the stiletto shoes she wore with her grey uniform, and changed them for trainers. Now she's busy mopping the floor, working her way down the corridor, picking up rubbish, closing windows.

'Not far to go,' I say.

'German?'

'English. I'm looking for a place to stay.'

'That's difficult. You won't find it.'

'And you, where do you live?'

She doesn't answer. I go to the toilet and wash rather grimly with a tiny bar of soap and my plastic razor. It takes a while in the cramped, dirty cubicle. I brush my teeth, using the last of my bottled water to rinse.

By the time I'm finished we have arrived. Since Samara the train has never been far from the Volga. Now we are close to its end at the Caspian Sea. The whole trip has taken about thirty hours and we have travelled more than twelve hundred kilometres. It's the Caucasus but we are still not particularly close to the mountains. They are another day's travel away, a little more to the south and west.

The end-of-the-line station isn't big. Everything about it is grey and lifeless, and on the street it's the same. I think perhaps the impression has something to do with the orientation of the building, a trick of topography. Natalya had kept reminding me of the fish market that sold twenty different types of sturgeon, and her mother had brightened when she saw me take a small cucumber from my bag and bite into it. 'You should see the cucumbers in Astrakhan,' she had said. 'Such cucumbers and tomatoes! Such water melons! And the taste!' I was ready to believe it, but where were these fruits, this incredible produce that was almost too good to be true? Where were these ripe tomatoes that smelt of paradise, these melons the size of beach balls?

I walk up a flyover past low-rise apartment blocks, dragging my suitcase on wheels behind me. Early morning traffic flows past without a break. There's nothing growing anywhere. It's all cement with rubbish over the verges. And then, at the top of the flyover, I see a market snaking along the road below; a streak of colour disappearing under a bridge. Clothes and household gadgets are laid on the ground on rugs, with rocks at each corner to hold the rugs in place.

But I can't get to the road from where I am. This lot of plastic stuff from China, straight off the container, is being sold on a different level to my level and there's no way to get down, not without going back to the station. To the other side of the flyover, at the end of a slip road, is a petrol station with two pumps and a shop. I buy a bottle of orange juice and ask the woman behind the counter how to get to town, and where the market is which sells the wonderful produce. She looks at me for a long time, as if my question was some kind of trick. Then shrugs her shoulders and points to a bus stop.

It's still early when the driver drops me outside the old kremlin. Beyond the gates, the cobbled courtyard with whitewashed stone walls is empty. There's a church to one side, and on an information board a print of a seventeenth century scene showing the busy river curling around fortified walls. The gilded belfries of the cathedral glitter in the morning sun, just as they do in the print. The whitewashed walls haven't changed either, but the river has gone. I walk through town, down the long empty avenues until I reach an open space with a view of cranes. The old sand banks are covered with concrete. Across the water is a darkly-wooded island, and let into the low wall of the promenade are steps leading to a floating pontoon where a tourist boat is moored, its sailing times posted on a wooden easel. A man, extraordinarily dressed up in a sailor's stripy suit, is cleaning the deck. He confirms that the timetable is correct, and that the boat will sail in twenty minutes, customers or no customers.

The mighty Volga, mother of Russian legend, laps heavily against the river wall, swirling brown and smelling of weed. Behind the trees the facades of the buildings are cracking, the windows dead. The riverside is deserted and apart from the spotlessly turned out crew the boat is empty, but this doesn't seem to matter. The white-painted iron gangway door is shut and we cast off, heading round and into the current. A crackly message welcoming visitors on board is relayed on the loudspeaker. I find myself a place on the upper deck below an awning, and order lunch with a glass of beer.

Soon the domes of the cathedral come into view. The steady pulse of the diesel engines carries over the splash and bump of waves. We motor under a bridge by a green-glass office building and then, as we turn into the main stream and follow through the bend, I see the first signs of life, pale skin and white scraps of towels: swimmers on the opposite bank, and a strip of clean sand running between tall reeds.

19

The popular Russian television drama, *Seventeen Moments of Spring*, was supposedly Putin's favourite film, and inspired him to become a secret agent. It begins with a shot of geese flying north in a V formation. The snow has gone but the buds have not yet opened. Sterlitz, a Russian spy working in Hitler's bunker during the last months of the war, is walking in the woods with an elderly lady, a friend. They comment on the winter, on the spring, and how the spring is like a victory over death.

'Isn't it?' asks the old lady taking a few steps forward.

Sterlitz looks to one side, frowns.

'I suppose you're right' he says.

And so they walk to the car and drive back to town. It's easy to imagine Putin loving this film. His father fought behind enemy lines in Estonia, his elder brother died during the blockade of Leningrad, and his mother was close to starvation. After the war he grew up in a small shared flat, part of an old stuccoed building overlooking a courtyard that was overrun with rats. In his autobiography Putin talks of his father as a silent hero and of himself as the indomitable survivalist, the kid who is able to learn from life's tough lessons. The film, like Putin's early life, is full of hair-raising challenges and moments of extreme danger, while the film's hero, Sterlitz, always manages to scrape through, his identity still undetected, his mission intact.

I'm sitting on a bench with my notepad on my knee in a run-down slum area of old wooden houses beyond the flyover that leads to the station. Acacia trees grow everywhere, their narrow leaves covered in a film of white dust. They sprout from decrepit brick footings, crowd blind alleyways, push through rotten roofs. Some have taken root in the middle of the street. You can smell the river close by.

I have a go at one of the Sudoku puzzles and then stop. My notebook is full of sketches and diary entries. I flip through and come to the place where you can write your name, address, and a reward sum. I think to myself: I had better fill it in. What if I lose it? There isn't much here, but you never know, it might turn out useful. I write $100 in the reward space and then begin to fill in other details, my name and address, my telephone number. I put my email at the bottom. The person who picks this notebook up will have everything they need to give it back to me.

I think: if I was Sterlitz I'd be more careful. And perhaps Putin is so careful because Sterlitz was so careful. Perhaps Nick would not be barred from travelling and working if Sterlitz hadn't been so careful. Or perhaps Nick would not be barred from travelling and working if Vyacheslav Tikhonov, the actor who played Sterlitz, hadn't been so good. History might have turned out quite differently if the secret agent in the old Mosfilm movie hadn't been so quietly attractive.

A message comes through on my phone from Olga, asking if I'm okay. Her concern seems a little strange to me, especially as there is nothing from Lyuba or the children. It occurs to me that the text might have been sent jointly, by both mother and daughter, as a way of keeping me out of the loop. A tactic to deal with the wandering husband and keep him thinking. I don't mind that, and in a way it makes little difference. It's true, after all. I'm wandering off to get certain things clear in my head. At the moment I'm trying to work out what is the acceptable thing to do or to say, and what is not. What the good reason for returning is. And I'm not sure yet.

I reply to Olga with a picture of the promenade, a view with a perspective that conjures up postcard images of holidays sensibly spent: a bench, the river wall, an empty esplanade. It's the sort of shot she would like, the sort of postcard-picture a dutiful son-in-law in an old-fashioned movie might send in good faith, before trouble strikes.

It's quiet and neglected here, like a wasteland, but there are also signs of people. A broken window has been boarded up, makeshift curtains are strung across an opening. In one of the houses, where the curtains don't shut properly, I see a framed photograph propped on a table. Yet it's hard to say what's lived in and what's not. Some of the houses are tumbling down, almost in ruins. Rubbish is piled up, spewing out through broken planks. Further up the street a side door hanging off its hinges is pushed open, and a man with tightly curled sand-coloured hair appears, balances the door back in position, and turns to leave. I notice a movement in one of the upper windows. A woman is staring at me from behind the dirty glass. I can make out her features very clearly, snub upturned nose, wide open eyes, pale eyebrows. The man is already halfway up the street walking with odd jaunty movements, one shoulder higher than the other. When I turn back the face in the window has gone. I walk over and push one of the rotten slats. There's an overgrown garden with a dilapidated barbecue made of bricks, a can of beer, a book lying open on the unlit barbecue, and an easy-chair with grass growing through it. High in the sky a buzzard hovers, small and dark in the bright sun.

20

It's midnight and the bus is hot and full. Other buses are parked outside this rest stop and there is a constant coming and going of people from a long hut. I take a walk with the others and buy a cup of sweet tea and a pastry from a vendor sitting on the ground near to the toilets. Back outside I begin some stretching exercises on the broken tarmac.

I left Astrakhan in a rush, almost a panic. Beyond the parking lot in all directions the night is absolutely black, as if we were gathered in the last still-living place on earth. This country used to live off caviar, now it's oil. Behind the town and towards the sea are the derricks, nodding to the rhythm of dollars, ripping up the earth just as the sturgeon were once ripped up – in a rush to life. Everything feeding off everything else. The same here as everywhere. The gentle massage of something living, working over something dead.

I follow the last of the passengers onto the bus and soon we are on the move again, climbing steadily up a long and gradual incline. I wonder what my panic was. Maybe just tiredness. Or maybe something to do with the town. Strange ideas to do with the past, not my own particular past but something different, as if one was able to dredge up information from a deep well of others' experience.

During the early years of revolution the Bolsheviks, under the command of Sergey Kirov, liquidated thousands of dock workers and factory workers in Astrakhan. The workers had convened illegally to discuss the problem of food shortages. First of all soldiers fired rifles into the air over their heads. A few minutes later they began firing into the crowd with machine guns. There was no screaming or shouting. The men threw themselves to the ground and when the firing didn't stop, they began running in all directions over the dead bodies. They were chased into back alleys and into buildings and shot. Out in the streets artillery pieces were used against them. Afterwards the troops rounded up as many workers as could still be found and put them under arrest in the town's prison, in cellars, and on barges and ships moored in the river.

Kirov telegraphed for more orders. Trotsky advised merciless retribution (for questioning the revolutionary authority). And so a second, worse wave of violence began. The captive men were taken out of the cellars and shot in compounds. Those on board the prison barges were trussed up and pushed over the side with stones tied to their heads. Corpses were piled up and taken out of town by night on wagons. Bodies fell off the wagons and were left on the streets where they were found by their families, blood soaked and bullet-ridden.

Five days later the cavalry was sent out to the surrounding villages and into the steppe to pick up those who had tried to escape. The roads were deep in slush and mud. It was March, and the Volga was thawing and un-crossable. Those who were found were brought back as traitors and shot.

The families of the workers were then made to attend the funerals of the soldiers who had died in the rounding-up operation, to sing hymns and say prayers for their souls, and to condemn their own husbands, brothers and fathers. The Red Cavalry, armed with whips and pikes this time, dragged them from their homes to take part. Afterwards the newspapers talked of revenge, and promised that the revolution would not forget.

In his book on the revolution, written while he was in exile in Mexico, Trotsky said it was in the dockyards of the south that its spirit first showed itself. Yet in a thousand pages of well documented and often first-hand history, there is no mention of this liquidation-incident. The huge book is written in the clear declamatory style of Marx, and seems interesting at first, though it soon becomes hard to read. Perhaps the clue to this lies in another smaller book, Trotsky's autobiography, also written in Mexico in the thirties. Right at the beginning of this other, autobiographical book, Trotsky relates quite honestly a moment from his childhood. He is with his mother on a visit to a neighbouring farm. There is a little girl with whom he spends time. The girl has gone and he is left alone in the upstairs bedroom. His mother appears, together with the girl's mother. In the middle of the floor is a puddle. Trotsky has wet himself, and his mother asks him whether or not he is ashamed. Without a moment's hesitation he denies any involvement, he's absolutely confident, and in this passing of the blame away from himself and onto the absent girl, he feels neither shame, nor guilt.

I have not heard from Nick, and I'm reluctant to bother Kheda yet. The continued safety of a human rights journalist in a place like Chechnya is not something to be taken for granted. Recent video footage on my phone shows her pleading with mothers of the Chechen fighters caught up in Syria for their safe return, so she should be all right for the time being. But in the world of reporting there are always two different angles right from the beginning, how it looks from the outside and how it is from the inside. In the interests of self-preservation and to continue doing her job effectively, Kheda has always worked within the regime's boundaries. She gives voice to stories, and when the stories end up in the world's press they might bring aid or justice to victims, or target wrongdoers and help bring the weight of a common morality down on their heads. But they also take on a life of their own that defines the world they come from, eventually forming a substitute world. Chechnya, when it is noticed at all, has become a distillation of violent repressions overseen by comic book villains, and nothing else.

Behind me the land seems to cling to the edge of a hole, unwilling to slip into darkness. In front of me, backs of heads wobble very slightly from side to side. Everyone has black hair, mountain people, sunburnt women wearing bright-coloured, patterned headscarves. I fall into a light sleep. Two hours pass, three hours. Finally I fall into a proper, deep sleep.

When I wake the sun is full and strong, like a searchlight in my eyes. By seven o'clock we have arrived in Pyatigorsk, where I buy a plastic pack of salami, a bottle of olives, and another ticket as far as Nalchik. The morning air has a sharp edge to it, and mountains poke up behind the rooftops.

Elbrus is close, but it can't be seen. Beyond the mountains are the vineyards and old tea plantations of Georgia. To the east the Caucasus range runs in a straight line to Baku, on the Caspian Sea. Elbrus is the highest mountain around, higher even than Mont Blanc - though there's no cable car to the top.

Up in the mountains the snow is in retreat. It has been for some years now and every season something or other is uncovered, empty shell cases, rusty insignia, belt buckles, helmets, whole artillery pieces. This is a part of the world where hubris founders at the extreme limit of empire. The Greeks imagined Prometheus here, tied to a rock and forever tortured beyond the reach of mortal man. The Romans pushed in from the west and gave up, the Persians and Ottomans came from the south, Russia from the north. They all reached their territorial limits here, and in 1942 it was no different. The vanguard of the German Sixth Army was on its way to Baku, to reach the oil fields, and an advance guard was sent to secure a way through. They got as far as Elbrus, on the summit of which (in a fit of enthusiasm which later sent Hitler into one of his carpet-chewing rages) they planted a swastika flag.

The bus heads off at two o'clock, following a river running high and fast between steep cliffs. It's a beautiful ride but the bus is hot and smells of exhaust, and I'm tired and keep falling asleep. Opposite me is a family, a father with his children by the looks of it, including a boy of fourteen or fifteen. The boy watches me with dark, amused eyes. I have one hand resting on my inappropriate luggage, one of those bags designed for fitting into the overhead lockers of an airplane, with a retractable handle and a zip pocket at the front, and small plastic wheels. My head is nodding. Whenever I wake there's the family and the boy opposite, and through the window another extraordinary view. The green mountain river foams over the rocky bed. Both banks are overgrown with sea buckthorn bushes which show bright orange with berries.

'Are they picked?' I ask the father of the boy.

'Oh yes!' he replies nodding his head and smiling, though I'm not sure he understands me.

The bushes continue all up the valley, showing the same orange berries. I drift off again, thinking of these bushes and of the berries that are almost ready for picking. I know about these berries, but it's a surprise to see them here. Olga used to have a bush in her old dacha and made a syrup with them every year. She would fill a thick glass jar and send it to us, wrapped in something soft to stop it from breaking. In those days she would spread the news amongst her friends, and then wait until someone was travelling out of Russia before giving them a package. Sometimes the carriers of these parcels stayed with us in London. More often than not they were in transit, and we would meet them at the airport, or pick up the packet from a third party at an unfamiliar address in a suburb of London we had never visited before. That was how it was in those days. All Russians abroad belonged to the same family, a network that held together through a kind of DIY-DHL. The packages were not usually presents. Mostly they were things which seemed essential, that you couldn't get in England. Or else, on the return run, it would be something essential that you couldn't buy in Russia. The important thing was the item's unique quality, its essence, though it seems to me now that these 'essential' items were never used after they were first unwrapped, and that behind the networking was a simple emigre isolation that needed to be worked through.

I zoom in on the bushes with my phone camera and take a joggy picture. It doesn't come out well. You can't tell what the orange smear is, and the dirty window of the bus makes it look foggy. I want to send the picture to Lyuba to remind her of the claims she made, not long after we first met, that sea buckthorn berries can cure EVERYTHING! At that time the berries formed a potent link with her past, a kind of jam-making solidarity with her old life and ways of doing things, and I was ready to believe her.

The driver pulls up near to a small bridge and gets out to make a phone call. His engine has overheated and he opens the bonnet to have a look, though he doesn't try to mend anything. After a while somebody arrives, and both men bend over and fiddle with the wiring. We wait for maybe a half hour, or forty minutes. Then the radiator is filled with water from the river, and we set off again.

Soon afterwards, the family sitting opposite get out. I would have liked their company all the way but there's nothing to be done, and after another hour the rest of the passengers are dropped off as well, and I'm on my own. Woods begin to crowd the valley, tall pine trees stand singly in the pastureland that comes right to the edge of the road. Further on, in what seems a random place high up in these steep alpine meadows, the driver stops and tells me to get out and walk. He points up the valley, and then turns and drives back towards Nalchik.

Towards evening I arrive at the bottom of a mountain of shale, an accumulation of frost-shattered shards of rock, thin and grey, that stretches upwards for as far as I can see. A rusty chair lift towers over the few wooden houses. This is the last stop for Elbrus, the end of the road where groups of enthusiasts used to gather in crowds and prepare for their ascent. There are two hotels under the shadow of the mountain. The first one is closed. I ring the doorbell and look through the front window for any signs of life. From the dimness of the lobby a large stuffed elk stares back out at me.

The second, less promising hotel, is still under construction. Scaffolding covers half of the building, but the door is open, and inside it's all tiles and smells of cleaning fluid. This time, when I ring the front desk bell a woman appears from upstairs and gives me the keys to a narrow, gloomy room on the second floor, with a window facing a wood yard.

21

It was raining when Lyuba arrived in England for good. I met her off the boat at Dover, in the evening. She came through with Boris and a suitcase. Boris had a tiny rucksack on his back with his toys. Lyuba wore a dark blue dress. I had no idea what was going to happen, or how we were going to support ourselves.

We went for a walk along the front. The rain had stopped, but everything was still damp and dripping. There was a palm tree and a fun fair, very quiet but still open. Boris wanted to go on the slide, and I took him up the steep metal stairs to the top of a monstrous chute that glistened damply in the glare of the funfair's single arc light. We slid down the shiny metal slope on pieces of coconut matting and got our trousers wet.

On the walk back to the car, I promised myself that I would not return to live at home with my parents, but it was a reckless promise without a plan. I was not prepared for a life of work. There was no way I could earn enough to support my new family. And where were we to go? How was I to find the money to rent a flat?

Since leaving school in Watford I had received money from my parents to live on. I had failed to get into music college, but got into art college instead. That was a turning point. The first time I entered a life drawing class on the foundation course in Amersham I felt as if I had entered a new life and didn't want to leave it. I worked hard and the following year I got on a course to study painting at the Royal Academy Schools. I moved up to London and rented a room in Swiss Cottage from an old university colleague of my father's, a Canadian who always seemed to be in the throes of another complicated love affair. His bedroom was also the living room, and I had to walk through it to get to my room. I would often meet his women, and they all seemed old and paranoid in the same way, one after another. But he was kind to me, and gave me a copy of Turgenev's *Sketches* with the picture of a young nobleman travelling by open coach through the Russian countryside, the same one that I have in my bag now. He gave me suppers, and took me to the movies to watch Visconti and Fellini.

I used to cycle to college, ate frugally, and had a student grant which was enough to get by on. I made no friends. In those days the Academy was very old-fashioned. Students were met at the entrance by the doorman in a tailcoat with a 'Morning Sir!' The signing-in book lay open on a desk next to the Venus de Milo, while just around the corner was a full sized cast of the Laocoön, its writhing snakes and pubescent victims dominating the old flag-stoned corridor lined with every sort of statue from antiquity. George Stubbs's flayed horse was positioned by the keeper's door opposite a row of skeletons. The entrance to the print studios was watched over by a twenty foot Hercules resting on a club, his big toe the size of a coffee cup.

Opposite the life drawing room was the Belvedere Torso. I spent most of my three years there trying to get this statue right, and each time I started on a fresh sheet of paper I believed it was the time, that every line would fall into place just as I dreamed it would. I wanted to be a great drawer. Picasso was dead (he died when I was in primary school) but his drawings lived on, and it was his drawings of casts that inspired me the most. I came out of college a little better at drawing but without a single idea in my head as to what to do next. I worked and even tried to show my work but without success. Perhaps I didn't want success. I could see the bargaining and the compromise and it didn't appeal to me, but after meeting Lyuba I tried harder. In between washing-up jobs, van-driving jobs, taxi jobs, and bar jobs, I worked on a series of large paintings. They were gloomy and depressive, and when they were finished I decided to photograph them at the seaside. We drove down to the big stretch of sand which runs along the Sussex coast at Camber. We had got to know this bit of coastline together, the dunes, the muddy, shallow sea. It was the place we always aimed for when we got a chance to take a day out.

There was a carpark with a cafe, and a single storey hut with a few gaming machines. In the middle of the carpark was a vending machine with a talking parrot and presents. Every time you put fifty pence in the slot the parrot nodded and said: *'I like the sound of money,'* in a strangled, parroty voice. Then the present fell out at the bottom. Boris used to like this machine with its mechanical talking bird, and its humorous ditty.

We took photos and then tied my pictures back onto the roof of the car. It was November and, as usual, we were struggling along without money. After feeding the parrot our last fifty pence we walked along the top of the dunes towards the golf course. That was when we saw the first of the sea buckthorn bushes. They stretched along the coast as far as you could see. It seemed miraculous that these 'completely Russian' bushes should be growing in England just near to a cafe which served 'All-Day-Breakfast' and frozen Cornettos. There was a continuous chirruping of small birds. The berries were bright orange and grew in clusters between needle-sharp thorns. We picked until it grew dark. Afterwards we made a point of returning each year when the first storms had blown over, and the berries were just starting to lose their colour and break open.

22

The air is thin. You cannot see a great deal under the mountain. The old lift stands empty in the deep morning shadow next to a small, swift flowing stream.

By seven thirty there are six of us waiting for it to creak into motion, three young climbers from Poland, a Bulgarian man, and a local climber with a pleasant open face who seems to be a guide for the Bulgarian. The closed car takes ten minutes to get out of the valley to the first lift station. From here we walk up a cinder track through an area of boulders, a confusion of blackish brown stones piled up on top of each other, some of them very large so that they tower over us like buildings. The path leads to a second, smaller chair lift, rusty like the first one, and unmanned. The guide is not sure whether someone will arrive to switch it on. It could be broken. The air is cold. Below us and behind us, chains of snow covered mountains stretch southwards. The Bulgarian is inclined to wait, the three mountaineers from Poland are uncertain. They are planning to spend two days acclimatising before attempting the summit and need to get up as high as they can on this first day. I look at the twin peaks, blunt and seemingly not too imposing, and then shake hands with them all, and set off on my own.

For the first hour the path is wide, laid with black volcanic stone and edged like a wall with huge boulders. This path comes to an end before the snow begins by a collection of rusty, padlocked containers. Here a series of smaller paths continue through the rock walls, like the beginnings of an elaborate cave system. Sometimes the paths open out unexpectedly, as paths in archaeological sites open onto excavations. There are more containers, rusty hulks in the last stages of decomposition, places of refuge for mountaineers that are now shut and abandoned. I follow a narrow path, past the last container, a cylindrical one that has been propped on stones to keep from rolling over.

The boulders also come to an end here. Beyond this point everything is white, a flawless, sparkling field that runs up at a slight angle. Sticks are planted in the snow, with footsteps following the sticks upwards. After half an hour of climbing I turn, and look back. Somewhere at the top of one of these ridges is a border where Georgia begins. Further south, beyond all these mountains, lies Iran.

I'm not well-equipped. My boots are just normal boots for trudging around the forest in, without crampons. I have no ice axe, or gloves. My jacket is from the clothing department of Sainsbury's, bought for £7 the day before I left. But I have sunglasses and sun cream. When I look up it seems as if the blue sky has become darker, pressing down heavily. To the east there appears to be another way to the summit, though it would mean leaving the trail. This way looks more beautiful and perhaps a little less steep. In this direction the snow-field has no distinguishing features, no rocky outcrops, hillocks, or ravines. To the south and west the mountains are brilliant white with blue serrated shadows. Due north is a large outcrop of exposed rock. The less-steep ascent curls upwards, beyond the eastern side of this rock. It looks empty and incredibly beautiful, this sheet-like slope and beyond, a slew of boulders.

After half an hour the trail and the sticks have disappeared behind the side of the mountain. There is no sound but the cold wind, not yet strong, and the crunch of my steps in the brittle ice layer that covers the snow. I am making my way slowly round the mountain, thinking of one thing and then another, everything unconnected and running in parallel with walking-rhythms indistinguishable from loneliness: the feel of cold air filling my lungs, the sense of my body moving underneath my clothes, the sound of crunching snow, of heavy breathing, and of nylon brushing against nylon.

Suddenly the ground gives way. Before I have time to think I am clawing at a wall of snow. Snow is in my mouth. I cannot see or move well. My arms are spread wide, and everything from my neck down is buried. I reach upwards and then keep still. I can feel my heart pounding, and at the same time it occurs to me that if

I move the ground might collapse again. I am still upright and there is still a hole of sky above, but I have no idea what is below.

I bring one leg up as far as it will go, wedge myself against the edge of the hole with my shoulders and thighs, and dig in with my toes, pushing upwards. I repeat this operation with the other leg, then wait for a moment. On the third try I manage to put an elbow onto the icy snow surface and pull myself up and out. I lie still, flat on the ice. It's very quiet. The sun is bright, arcing across the snow, making it sparkle. I slide away from the hole on my stomach using my hands as paddles. When I'm ten feet away, I stand and shake the snow from my clothes.

For a while I cannot think straight. The snow plain stretches in all directions, absolutely uniform, treacherous, covering crevasses, fissures, ice holes. The snow could have collapsed anywhere along the route, or in any direction around me. I wonder if this is the trouble I was to fall into, the dutiful son-in-law who sent pictures of the esplanade in Astrakhan? It could make good comedy. A farce, perhaps. Why did he leave the trail? Was he looking for something? Could it be he was attempting to climb the mountain without a warm jumper or gloves? If my notes were found it might help, though whoever it was who found them would likely come to the conclusion that I was simply unsound, and had left the trail as a way of escaping life altogether.

My tracks have roughed out a curved line around the mountain. I walk slowly with my arms ready to stretch out if the ground falls away again. It's midday by the time I reach first base and the end of the smaller, broken chair lift. There is no sign of the Polish mountaineers or of the Bulgarian and his guide. Here there are more containers, including one of those cylindrical ones that seems to have been removed from an oil tanker. Once more, everything is dominated by a deposit of massive dark boulders. Beyond this place of refuge the mountain looks more desolate. The wind has picked up. A man walks down from the boulders, an oldish bearded man with an educated face. He looks a little crazy and pleased to see me in the way people are who haven't had company for a while. We greet each other and he soon finds that I'm a foreigner, and moreover

English. He is surprised by this, genuinely amazed, as if the pent up questions of years gone by were waiting to come out. For a moment he is speechless.

'There!' he says finally, gesturing towards the rocks behind us. I look up and see a small orange tent half hidden in a nook.

'Have you been up?' I ask.

He doesn't reply to my question but looks across at the line of rusty shelters.

'Tomorrow I will see if there is some space.'

I look upwards. There seems to be a kind of mist or smoke gathering around the summit.

'You see?' he is pointing upwards again, where I am looking.

I follow his finger, but I can't see anything in particular.

'Climbers!'

Still I can't see. Maybe my eyes aren't so good. I look at his watery grey eyes, bloodshot and tired-looking. Perhaps they are super-keen.

'You see the rocks?'

Quite a way up there is an uneven dark patch. I wonder whether this is what he's on about.

'To the left! Can you see?'

I look harder at the whiteness to the left of the rocks. Again there seems to be nothing there. And then I spot a number of tiny dots. I count six, spread unevenly in a line heading for the top. Tiny specks, much smaller than I'd been expecting. You cannot even see them move. I turn towards my companion to thank him for pointing them out, but he seems distracted, as if he's late for an appointment. He's lost interest in me and wanders off.

I have no warm jumper, no supplies or sleeping bag. It's time to get back down. Before I leave I walk over to the lonely man in his orange kagool, thin and wiry – the sort of physique that would do well when food gets scarce. I want to wish him well, to say goodbye. He looks upwards at the dots again. We both look for a while. He tells me that it's fourteen hours from here to the summit and then down again. I don't ask him again whether he will attempt it, or whether he has already done this. He has become distracted once more, and I have to leave. The wind has picked up and the sun has lost its warmth. The temperature is dropping as I head down, following the path between the sticks this time, towards base camp and a lift that will take me to the village.

23

A month after my father's death I had a dream we were both walking in the mountains. In the dream my father was wearing a knapsack and taking his leave of me. He had to go, and I wasn't to follow. He walked along a narrow roped bridge over an abyss of spray and rocks, and when he was on the other side he turned and waved, and at that moment I realized he had gone for good, and that I wouldn't see him again.

The Alpine setting of the dream came from a family holiday we once took in Switzerland. We had climbed a mountain path together. It wasn't as steep or as perilous as the mountain that lies behind this hotel now, but there was a sheer drop and in the valley below, a kind of mist or cloud. My father suffered from vertigo and couldn't go on. I remember the sick look on his face as he swayed on his long legs, and my feelings of concern and impatience as we prepared to return back down.

I think of this dream, as I lie under the bedsheets looking up climbing accidents online. My ankles are sore. I don't feel capable of going much further. Perhaps my father had similar problems with his feet. He liked to keep his own problems out of the way, and when the problems were general he often used to do the same. When he talked of Russia he relied on information that was not political. He would talk of Prokofiev's emotional return to Moscow in 1936, and with wide-open eyes explain its inevitable nature, as if the beauty and nobility of the composer's homeland was laid out in front of him in the kitchen. Or he would mention Stravinsky's yearning for Russia as an exile in Paris and, with head bowed, and eyes half closed (because he wasn't so keen on Stravinsky), would relate the scorn shown by Stravinsky towards those Westerners who liked passing judgement on things Russian, forgetting for a moment the scorn Stravinsky also heaped on the Soviet establishment when they dared to criticise his music.

I reach down and pull on my feet, stretching the ankles in the hope they will improve by morning. Through the small window the tree-covered slopes are half sunny and half in shadow. Tomorrow I'm going to Grozny, Chechnya's capital, rebuilt after the years of war and struggle for independence from Russia that ended in failure. An email has come in from Kheda, and it seems she's expecting me. I haven't told Olga, or Lyuba. Grozny has always been a setting for untimely ends and of grief, and it would only make them concerned. The mountains here have been the scene of many troubles in war and in peacetime, and Russia has always been involved. I remember the first time I watched the 1967 mountaineering film, *Vertical*, shot not far from where I'm staying now, and being surprised by the flashbacks in the film - the shells exploding in the snow, the machine guns poking up from black rocks.

When Anna Politkovskaya was murdered (on Putin's birthday in 2006), there was an outcry that reached the pages of the foreign press and was nurtured by literary commentators. Here was a woman who spent her best years documenting the horrors of war in Chechnya and in the process uncovering the corruption of the Russian occupying forces. She was shot as she walked from the lift outside her flat.

When Boris Nemtsov was murdered, in 2015, there was another outcry: here was a legitimate contender for the presidency, gunned down in the centre of Moscow. This time the outcry was orchestrated by the Kremlin: 'How could it have happened? What have we come to?' And: 'We will find these murderers if it's the last thing we do...'

Six weeks later the state department traced the hitmen back to the Caucasus. Two Chechens confessed (and later retracted their confessions). One Chechen blew himself up in his apartment in Grozny, where he had been followed and surrounded by special forces.

Chechnya is the enclave that forms a backdrop to a thousand

cover-ups, double dealings and political strangulations. Here the wildest and most troubling claims have been made, and nobody seems able to care any more.

24

Over Christmas and into the new millennium the war in Chechnya entered a more bloody phase. I was celebrating modestly with Lyuba and her parents in Moscow (I remember being very pleased with a new coat I had recently bought in London, a three-quarter length sheepskin coat, quite warm. All the photos of this time show me wearing it.) We were struggling at that time, carrying on in our damp flat in south London, still uncertain as to how people were able to live so well in expensive apartments, in more fashionable parts of town. On Lyuba's first visit to London she stayed with Zinik and his wife, Nina, in their flat in Lewisham. Later Zinik moved to Hampstead, to a flat in a big white house on Haverstock Hill. We often visited, driving across town for a Sunday lunch and trying to appear, if not successful, then at least not mired in the money problems we found ourselves facing on a day-to-day basis.

It was quiet in Moscow with Olga and Nikolai. There was the usual supper with vodka and small snacks on the table, pickled mushrooms, caviar, selyodka, black bread and butter. There was borscht, a breaded fish of some sort, and a large, sticky cake. Olga had prepared plenty of food, and afterwards we walked in the snow to the Sputnik cinema where there was an outdoor party with more food and bunting hanging between the street lights. There is a photo of us standing together, Lyuba with her head turned from the camera, and myself in the three-quarter length sheepskin coat with a big smile on my face. Surprisingly to me now, it shows somebody who looks quite content, and perhaps this has something to do with the coat. Here is a man, no longer young, who has got through the most trying times, and has managed to buy for himself (for perhaps the first time) a coat that makes him look okay, which is to say reasonably prosperous. This is not to say I was well-off, but that prolonged effort had made it possible to appear so, and to disguise my real position.

Salman Rushdie wrote of an age when a writer could ignore the bigger picture and be thought none the worse for it, when Jane Austen might write of a soldiers' camp in Brighton, and talk of the scarlet uniforms without mentioning Napoleon. I was bound up with work in London and hadn't realised that Russian planes were bombing Grozny over the millennium period. I didn't know Nick well at that time, and wasn't aware he was covering the Chechen war and interviewing rebel commanders in bombed out hotels while we clinked glasses around the table in Aviamotornaya. Or that General Kvashnin had ordered one apartment block after another to be razed in Grozny, one block a day, in the kind of lesson the Romans practiced on their enemies – burn cities to the ground, then plough the fields with salt to prevent their return. Nick told me later that the Russians telephoned in advance with instructions as to which block was going to be bombed on a given day, to give time to evacuate. The Chechen fighters sandbagged the cellars and basements, and in hidden-away mountain villages they regrouped and recuperated.

Buildings were bombed into heaps of rubble. Entire areas were wiped out. Sometimes rows of tenements were only half destroyed so that, taken together with the other half-wiped-out buildings, the dust clouds, and the piles of miscellaneous detritus, the town began to look like those fantastically imagined scenes of antiquity drawn by Piranesi and Guardi.

There is a strange beauty to the photos of this war when they show people carrying on with their lives while everything crumbles around them – a young mother pushing a pram through broken streets, an impromptu shop set up on a table with a backdrop of smouldering, charred ruins. But you don't have to go far to see images that document the un-heroism which collected on the war's rotten underside all the time: the intimate snapshots of torture, the young sadists smiling and the victims who are still alive. And it was only later, when the reports started to filter through, that people began to get an idea of what lay behind the many low-key photos that were always being shown during these years, the checkpoints along the road manned by hungry paranoid recruits, the broken-down military vehicles, the piles of shell casings, the empty villages, the cratered highways, the skinny kids with gappy teeth, the bulky, hirsute commanders almost bursting through the seams of their flak jackets.

•••

My ankles have recovered enough to walk back down the road from the hotel, dragging my suitcase with its small wheels across the rough tarmac. To either side the pine trees are thick, healthy, tall. A small mountain river runs first on one side of the road, and then on the other. It's seven in the morning and the sun has not yet risen over the tall peaks. The whole valley is in shadow, but it seems as if it's going to be a hot day. I'm wearing shorts and a t-shirt and my tall Russian forest boots. An hour later I join a group of fifteen people who are gathered at the end-of-the-line bus stop under a large pine tree, waiting to be taken back to town.

It's hot by the time we reach Nalchik. The mountains are behind us, and crowds are milling around in a great confusion at the terminus. Once I have found what seems to be the stop for Grozny I stay put. If there is a bus I don't want to miss it. But there isn't a bus, and nobody quite knows whether there will be one or not.

A queue is forming with its own hard-to-understand logic. People arrive and then leave again. Some arrive as if they have been waiting for a long time already. Others turn up and it's obvious they know hardly any more than me about what's happening. They look around with worried expressions. They ask questions, then set themselves in front of me. I feel less worried than they look. But then I have nothing to worry *about*. I don't know where I am going to stay, or what I am going to do. I have just one thing on my mind, a vague disquiet that is summed up by the word Grozny.

The bus, when it finally gets going, is another small one, like a large transit van with seats and one sliding door. It's hot and there are lots of bags, but there is just room for everyone. I am crammed in at the back, my bag between my sweating knees, my hands in my lap, my shoulders turned in to take as little space as possible.

As we leave the mountains behind, the road becomes steadily less interesting. The flat landscape looks plain and characterless. We are driving through farmland, but there are also industrial warehouses, small villages, factory chimneys. The road is new, with bright yellow markings and galvanised crash barriers. In my travels across Russia I have never seen anything like this. There are roundabouts with brand-new traffic signs, white curbs, glistening tarmac. Mile after mile it's the same. Every so often we stop and exchange a few passengers from inside with a few waiting on the roadside. There is a good, jolly atmosphere shared amongst everybody in the bus except for the woman sitting right next to me, who seems bothered and keeps fidgeting.

Nick has replied to my text. He tells me that Kheda will meet me in Grozny. The eyes of my fellow passengers have begun to crease and close in the heat. Arms are draped over nylon laundry bags that are stuffed so hugely, not one tiny thing more would fit.

The further from the mountains we get, the more the woman next to me fidgets. She makes bad-tempered jerks of her body, and as soon as a space becomes available she moves with difficulty around all the luggage and sits with her back to me, shaking herself in disgust. I look across at my two immediate neighbours. I am expecting surprise, maybe even an explanation for what has happened, but the young men stare back at me stonily. They have the same slick black hair, paisley-patterned shirts, greasy chinos tightened with thin leather belts, shiny shoes.

We are close to Grozny, though there is still no evidence of war, nothing except for this obviously brand-new road running through the scrappy countryside. The offended woman gets off the bus with a great huffing and puffing, and enormous, exaggerated movements of her shoulders, as if she was struggling through something repulsive, but without looking at me. And then it's the last stop, the terminus. A kind of dusty corral, with a eucalyptus tree in the corner. When I am on the road with my bag, the two men approach me.

'What's that?' I ask.

One of them stretches forward and slaps my knee, then he waves his hand backwards and forwards in front of my face. The other explains:

'You shouldn't wear short trousers!' he says.

At first I don't understand what he means.

'It's forbidden!' He looks at me without the slightest trace of humour on his face. Then he looks down at my tall boots again, raises his hand in another warning gesture, and leaves with his friend.

It's boiling hot in the square. Bark is peeling off the eucalyptus tree and onto a bench. Dust blows up off the dried earth. Everything is covered in dust, the car windscreens, the tree, the one-storey buildings.

I root around in my bag for the bottle of water and then go and wait in a bit of shade.

Nick has arranged for me to meet with Kheda here at the depot, and warned me to look out for someone who bears an uncanny resemblance to the artist, Tracy Emin. I know what Tracy looks like, and I have some grainy video footage of Kheda, so I guess I have some idea of who I'm waiting for. But now I wonder how he has introduced me to Kheda, and what he has told her to expect. I glance down at my illegal bare skin, at my knees (Verboten!) and at the bleached hairs that sprout from my thighs (Absolut Verboten!!) and at my tall Russian-issue boots with the laces already beginning to fray.

At last Kheda turns up. She looks nice, amused. Pleasant. She hustles me into a taxi and takes me to an apartment block where I am to be introduced to a class of children. It's her English class, but before meeting them she shows me to a side room with the window blinds pulled shut, and asks if I can change into long trousers. She closes the door and I sit and undoe my boots in the dark, and then feel for my belt buckle in the bag and pull on my jeans.

After the lesson we are taken by the driver for a tour of the city. We stop at Grozny's new mosque. For as far as you can see there are the same composite paving blocks, interlocking in a wavy pattern. The mosque has a green dome and yellow sandstone walls. Everything is new. Everything is very large. Apartment blocks have been built in the exact style, and on the same foundation lines, as those old ones levelled by Russian bombers. A banner with 'Thank you Ramzan!' written across it, hangs from the windows of one of the brand-new housing developments opposite the mosque. If you didn't know what's happened here, you would never guess.

It turns out that the taxi driver is also a bridge engineer. He chain smokes Lucky Strikes, and tells me all about the history of his country. He says Russia has always been the oppressor, while Chechnya has always been the saboteur. To understand the history of Chechnya you have to think of the geography, and of the mountains that run west-east from the Black Sea to the Caspian Sea. He says that it's enough to look at a map and read the names to understand that something has gone wrong: Dagestan, Ingushetia, North Ossetia, South Ossetia, Abkhazia, Chechnya. All these territories lie to the north side of the mountains and with the exception of South Ossetia have long been subsumed into greater Russia. On the other side of the mountains are the two newly independent countries of Georgia and Azerbaijan. The border between these two countries and the line of smaller Russian territories, runs up and down all along the tops of these mountains. You can step all over it and nothing will happen. It's just snow. Below the snow, clean volcanic detritus. Places of thin air, mountain foxes, eagles, ibex, and repositories for the bones of mountaineers.

Blue curls of smoke hang over the dusty dashboard. He waits while his words sink in, gives me a sideways glance. He likes the idea of geography informing the history. He tells me that from these snowy wastelands, where the bones of mountaineers rest, Azerbaijan slopes down southwards and eastwards to Iran and the Caspian Sea, while Georgia slopes down southwards and westwards to Turkey and the Black Sea. These two countries, along with Armenia which is wedged between them, form the South Caucasus, or what used to be called the Transcaucasus. He takes one hand from the steering wheel and sketches out these territories with his arm as if they were bulky things one could only just carry, that were difficult to get one's hands all around.

Georgia has an ancient Christian legacy. He tells me this with one finger held in the air, pausing for a moment like a fortune-teller. It was touched by the Roman empire when Russia was still an empty wilderness. Later, under the Tsars, it was seen as a prize worth fighting for, a wine growing paradise that stretched to the sea with wooded slopes protected from the north by rugged mountains.

On the other hand Azerbaijan was already old when the first Georgian kings adopted Christianity. It was less defined, more empty. It felt the influence of Europe less, it was wide open to Asia, and it had oil. Towards the end of the nineteenth century the Nobel brothers made enormous fortunes here. Oil cans were delivered all over Russia, all with the same red script and Nobel mark. The Rothschilds made fortunes here too. For a long while the Caspian Sea was the sticky centre of a great oil game that was played out over the whole world.

Chechnya was always in Russia's way, and when Russia came through, Chechnya rebelled. It harried the imperial troops who moved between their forts along the supply lines. It resented their arrival, though often there was nothing that could be done about it. Bargains were made, accommodations arrived at. Chechen leaders who rebelled were hunted down and killed, their villages burnt. Russia was not going to leave, and it needed to keep the routes through to the southern Caucasus open. Its tactics were heavy handed and brutal. The Chechens were forced into a role of subject peoples, their houses used as officer's billets, their flocks and crops used to feed the troops.

We are on the way out of town. He wants to show me something he has built, his contribution to the country. On the way through the low hills he tells me of the Chechen people's lowest moment, when they welcomed the Bolsheviks as liberators in 1917.

Two years later Stalin, in his role as regional chairman, subjugated them once more. Then, during the war with Hitler, he crushed and dealt with Chechnya in such a way that it would never rebel again. The entire Chechen population was deported in lorries and trains eastwards, to work in the empty desert lands. Those who resisted were shot. Men, women, children, the very old, everybody suffered the same fate. In 1956, during Khrushchev's so-called thaw period, the deportees took the opportunity given to all displaced peoples in the USSR to return home. His own family were among them.

And what about the latest war? What was he doing? Where was he? Kheda taps my shoulder from the back seat. The engineer lights up another cigarette and points to a bridge ahead, a small concrete one about twenty feet across that looks as if it had been there for years. Then he points to his own chest and nods. We drive a little more and then turn off down a track to a place where a metal pipe opens into a trough. Green-grey water pours continuously, hot and slimy on your skin, smelling faintly of rotten eggs. It runs over the edge of the trough and becomes lost in a stony ravine.

During the three years before she was murdered, Anna Politskaya reported on the first two Chechen wars and turned her dispatches into books that make grim reading. She wrote about the endless barbarities committed by the occupying forces, the robbery, the kidnap, rape and murder, the torture and the extortion, the beating up of old people, the forcing of people to do foul acts for entertainment, the ransoming of beaten-up children, the ransoming of corpses, the pointless vandalism of the inside of people's houses, the everyday moronic stupidity, the cowardly treacherous acts, the vindictive behaviour, the arbitrary cruelty.

Kheda used to talk of Natalya Estemirova, who headed up the Memorial movement in Grozny and was abducted on the street, on the way to an early morning meeting. She was close to Kheda and with each story uncovered would tell her of how difficult it was, and of how she felt a noose slowly tightening. Finally the order was given. Natalya was waiting for a bus. An unmarked car drove up and some heavies got out as if to ask a question, before grabbing her arms and hustling her into the back seat. Witnesses heard screams, but nobody followed the car. Natalya was taken to the forest and shot. Later her body was dumped near to the road, on the edge of town.

25

I lie in this made-up bed, a little window up high, a brass-effect ceiling fan, photographs on the table. Something is not right. I make sure my pyjamas are done up, and go to the bathroom. The kitchen is as it was after supper, with crumbs on the table. All the windows in this low house are small and high up – perhaps that's what has been bothering me. Kheda's husband, Misha, made an effort to be friendly last night. He's a typical southerner, dark thick hair, dark eyes, olive skin. He was a policeman, now he gets up late. On the couch is a pile of bulging cardboard folders. There is a faint whiff of old socks.

Maybe I should have asked Misha what his duties used to involve. Or maybe not. Kheda has to be careful about the past, about her plans, and what she is doing right now. She says she is being watched, followed, and I'm not surprised. When we sat down to lunch in the back room of a cafe yesterday, a group of kids trailed in after us and took a table close by. They kept quiet and didn't look over, but it was enough to make Kheda uncomfortable.

When Nick was here he interviewed the family of Umar Israilov, the former soldier who was shot dead in Austria just before he was due to give evidence implicating the governor of Chechnya, Ramzan Kadyrov, in the torture of prisoners. Israilov had prepared testimony which described his arrest and imprisonment in a boxing club. He talked of the other prisoners with him, of how they were tied up and beaten for long periods. How they were sodomized with a broken shovel handle. How he himself was tied to the exercise bars and electrocuted. How Kadyrov wandered through in the evenings to oversee the process, punching, kicking, helping with the electrocution, talking with the victims in measured calm tones as if they had been having a quiet drink in a downtown bar. His testament mentions how Kadyrov then walked to another corner of the gym, away from the prisoners tied up with blood running across the equipment, and played pool with his officers.

Treatment centres have begun to appear in town since the official end of the Second Chechen War, and they are full with people who do not understand how to deal with the symptons of their own trauma. Patients taken to these Centres for Islamic Medicine are diagnosed with evil spirits: an evil genie has entered their bodies and must be exorcised. The patient is led into a room, put onto a bed and beaten with sticks. Excerpts from the Koran are shouted into their ears.

It turns out that Kadyrov also has an evil genie bottled up inside him. He admits this openly. He goes to one of these new centres, gets beaten with sticks and has the Koran shouted at him. Afterwards he feels that the genie has been beaten up a bit. He feels better.

There is a television in the room where my bed has been made up. For a long while I watch a film, an epic by the looks of it. The actors are familiar. One of them has been a great favourite in Russia for years. Handsome but a little rough, strong and irresistible, he rides a white horse. A little later he stubs out a half smoked cigar, crushing the big expensive remnant in a gesture of languid resolve. It is a film of set pieces, one after another, extraordinary and beautiful, and yet a mishmash of lots of other films too. I have seen this actor wearing the same white suit, I have seen him crushing this cigar before, and I have seen his trunk before, then, as now, full of important documents hurtling across the steppe on the back of an open carriage drawn by black horses, their manes flowing in the wind. And now comes another surprise, Marcello Mastroianni, Fellini's favourite actor, walks into the film straight into a peasant hut. A few moments later he is visiting a bank in a prosperous provincial town – a gentleman in trouble, or so it seems. He looks older, more flaccid, soft at the edges, less of a man. The mannerisms he perfected in Fellini's films have settled into a form of weakness, and evoke only a terrible weariness.

I switch channels and settle on a slide show of nature films, showing the beauty of Chechnya's rivers and mountains and fields.

A river rushes over boulders. A deer stops to drink, waits, drinks again. A water droplet moves down the furrow of a leaf. The sun rises over the steppe majestically. A flock of birds streams past the camera, on and on, as if there was no end to them. God is here. God is in all of this. And now we see a young woman with a heavy expression, a kind of teacher dressed in black with a veil, though her face is showing. She talks of Islam, of Allah and his greatness.

Near the centre of town, somewhere high up in one of the new skyscrapers watched over by Allah, is a penthouse suite donated by Kadyrov to Gerard Depardieu. A gift from the town of Grozny to France's most noble actor. Probably he has never used it. Or maybe he's there now, lying on a good strong bed, his enormous body swelling the sheets, his eyes shut, his nose dilating imperceptibly with each breath.

26

There are soldiers on the train, not from one of the elite special forces or private militias by the looks of them, but regular troops on leave. They loll about on the slatted seats like any crowd of young men, pleased to be going home. I look at my map and trace the thin black line of the railway from Grozny to Astrakhan and then across to Rostov-on-Don. It cuts the troublesome Caucasus off from Russia very neatly, from the Caspian Sea to the Sea of Azov, just to the north of the Black Sea. The Black Sea is back in fashion for holidaying Russians, the place to go for the sun, just as it used to be in the old days when people joked that the only way out of the Soviet Union was vertically, up to the moon. It's no longer so fashionable to go abroad. The government is campaigning in the interests of self-preservation. Crimea has been reclaimed by Russian bikinis, its hot sands regulating the heartbeats and warming the skin of those loyal to Putin.

We are travelling up to Astrakhan again, back through bandit country. The train left an hour ago, at six in the evening. Kheda dropped me at the station, where we said goodbye quietly and quickly. That was the sort of place it was - the booted and blue-suited policemen walked around thuggishly, smiling while everyone else kept quiet and spoke only when necessary in short, scared sentences. You could see the surprise in the policemen's faces, as if they couldn't believe their game was working. The whole place cowed, everybody whispering and fearful.

I talk for a while to one of the soldiers sitting near me. He's quieter than the rest, good-looking, intelligent-looking. It turns out he's an officer on the way home to see his wife and her parents. He has kind eyes, a nice smile, he speaks German and English. I try to imagine him involved in one of the million corrupt deals, the gangster-like arrangements to keep the troubles festering for dirty profit, and the stories of foul thuggery which always circulated in Russia and abroad. But it doesn't work. I simply can't make the connection.

He returns to his friends and I hunch myself in the corner and get out the book Kheda passed me at the station, *KGB: Yesterday, Today, Tomorrow.* The light is fading, and for a moment it looks as if the country through the windows has been shot in sepia, everything a little hazy and tired-looking

27

The father of Baal Shem Tov, founder of the Hasidic line of Jews, imparted some wisdom to his son on his deathbed: a person should fear no one and nothing except God; a person (a Jew) should love all Jews whoever they are, and whatever they do.

He came from a tribe who had settled in the Don region, in the fertile area which begins where we are now, just a few yards from the train windows. One of his descendants, Yuri Bashmet, studied in the conservatoire in Rostov-on-Don, where this train terminates. In 2012 Yuri visited Van Walsum Management, the agency which represented him in London with offices near to Waterloo Bridge. He was tired, but relaxed. Despite the grey rawness of London he felt very well, as if everything had come into sharp focus. It was ten thirty in the morning and the staff were particularly attentive, running around making sure everything was comfortable and that it looked welcoming. They fussed around him, fawned on his every word, smiled and laughed at his wry observations. They sat him down on the sofa by the plants. What did he want? They would go to the end of the world to please him. Yuri Bashmet was a great artist, one of the extraordinary musicians of his time. An angel. He sat down in his street-kid way, making himself comfortable on the sofa with knees apart, and settled on a cold beer. The director grinned and asked him which sort. Any sort – but make sure it's cold! And so somebody was dispatched to the Tesco Express in a great hurry for a six pack of Stella. Jews and non-Jews in the office, and especially the girl who had to go out and pick up the beer, were outraged. Cans of cold Stella? At ten thirty in the morning? What kind of a degenerate behaved like that?

The soldiers have left the train. Most of them last night, and the last group this morning. We are approaching the broad, flattish, heroic landscape of the Don. On its opposite bank, fifty miles further on, between the towns of Mariupol and Donetsk, a war is festering in the east of Ukraine. The empire of Russia wants to keep out the American wolf that keeps appearing at the forest's edge grabbing lambs, and those who welcome this wolf into their home are traitors and enemies. Delinquents proclaim this and that. Opinions veer to one side or the other, and everybody is full of passion, convinced that the other side has it wrong. Nobody is immune: the educated, the simple, the devious, the well-meaning humanists.

My father talked of Russia when he was dying. He was delirious, said strange things, and made all sorts of claims. I used to visit him in hospital in Watford, travelling up by car from London. It was October and the leaves were turning. You could see them from his ward on the fourth floor. Perhaps he shouldn't have ended up in hospital. During his last days it might have been better if we could have taken him home, but to take him would have meant unhooking all the tubes, and giving up the possibility of using the emergency equipment if it was needed. He became thinner. His tongue dried up, and he refused to eat. The doctors remained upbeat. If there was a chance to keep him alive a little longer, they wanted to take it.

He told me that the past was the future, and that the future was behind us. He said that he hadn't got long, and that it was time to tell things as they were. One evening he explained that there was one thing, one extremely tiny thing that God couldn't see, and that in spite of his infinite wisdom there was still one detail missing. Or perhaps in His infinite grace there was still one too many things, out of all the infinite things that were good, something that wouldn't fit into place however many times you might try.

A week before he died he became delirious. He talked of the frog he could see balanced on my head. He expressed fear that it would shit on my head and told me to go to the other side of the bed, away from the bomb that had been planted by the Russians. He explained that if a person married an Austrian there would be continual war, that Princess Diana was burned on the fifth of November, that Napoleon was born in Brighton, that the Eucharist would continue for a thousand years, and that all pain comes from

Russia. He begged me to look after my firstborn daughter, Leila, and saw a dragon creeping up the wall, beating with its wings. 'Look!' he said. 'I'm counting the beats it makes, this segment thing...'

He died at five o'clock in the morning. His funeral was held some weeks later. Arrangements needed to made. Everybody had to be told. The undertaker told me that bodies keep for much longer than they used to because of all the preservatives in the food we eat. They dressed him up in his white suit, and did something to make his face appear less completely dead. My mother resented this but didn't say anything because the manager of the crematorium who had provided the funeral services was known to her, he was a tenor in the choir, and had been trying to do a particularly good job.

For a week my father lay in bed and my mother slept by his side. Then they took him to the funeral parlour and put him in the cold room, from where he was wheeled out, by appointment, for those who wanted to get a last look at him before the service.

...

I am trying to stop falling asleep by the time we arrive in Rostov-on-Don. We pass buildings which, even in my sleepy state, look quite different from anything I have seen so far. This is a city of the south, like Toulouse or Naples. The sun has flooded the streets and baked the walls leaving something permanent.

From the station I make my way into town looking for somewhere to stay. It feels almost like a European town but there are no hotels to be seen, nowhere to book into off the street, no vertical banners with names and stars. I'm directed uptown towards a modern high rise near the town hall square and the music academy. Somewhere here is the institute where Solzhenitsyn studied for his math's degree, and behind the windows facing the square, in one of those practice rooms, or perhaps all of them at one time or another, Yuri Bashmet worked through Schradieck and Kreutzer before stunning everybody in the recital hall with his Schubert.

The hotel is dull, new. I meet two hookers on the way up in

the lift, one of them smiles at me invitingly while the other stays serious. When the doors open they step smartly out. Perhaps they aren't hookers. Well, they're girls, nice-looking and on some kind of date, that's for sure.

I want to walk to the other side of the river to find a place to swim. Here in Rostov it's fine to wear my high, army-styled boots with short trousers. Nobody cares. We're beyond the mountains and back in Russia again, and nobody will twitch and shake themselves in disgust at the sight of my bare knees with their golden brown hairs. Two trolleybuses pass in different directions, like mirror images or double gates opening, and beyond them, on the other side of the street past the tramlines and overhead cables, is Detsky Mir, the toy shop I used to love so much when I first arrived in Moscow.

Then it had seemed like an Aladdin's cave of treasures, partly because the exchange rate had been such that I could afford anything. The children's toys piled up for sale in massive quantities were strange and different. There were musical gadgets, clockwork toys, toys with mathematical challenges, references to unknown traditions, sporting equipment for games I didn't know, New Year decorations like our Christmas decorations but invented in different styles. Paper chains and complicated tissue chandeliers. Piles of the most beautiful red plastic stars I had ever seen.

I buy a Rubik's Cube for Miles, and a jumper for Daisy. Then I put my baseball hat on because it's become hot outside, and walk down towards the grand sweep of the Don. The town is full of empty, boarded-up buildings, many of them for sale, but it feels more mellow than run down, a place of past grandeur and luxury with balustraded terraces like the terraces in Rome, overgrown and unkempt gardens, and steep streets with arched entrances leading to quiet communal courtyards.

I make my way along the embankment towards the bridge. It takes a long time to cross, and on the other side at the bottom of the spiral steps is a wasteland, with bushes and an unmade road leading to the river. Maybe there is something down here, a sandy beach, somewhere to lie down.

The golden globes of the cathedral shine on the opposite bank like the baubles that used to be piled up in Detsky Mir at New Year. The docks are further down the river, and you can see cranes poking up from behind the poplars in the distance. A sagging chain-link fence runs along the side of the concrete bridge supports to a low building, where the road turns into the trees. A dog appears at the bend, runs a little way towards me and then stops short and begins barking. A man is looking through the bushes. He's some way off but there's no mistaking the hostility. He seems to be waiting for something unpleasant to happen. I wander to the side of the road, as if I was interested in something there. A flower. I bend down, straighten up, and then make as if I am looking at the river, but a little away from where I know the man is standing. Then I turn and walk back to the bridge.

28

I have come the back way, over the sea. Kerch is behind me. Feodosia is behind me. I'm heading for Sudak through the wide open country of Crimea. The emptiness stretches for as far as you can see, and in the low hills the beginning of a story is taking shape, one that has been gathering there for a long time. I feel absurdly pleased with myself for having come this far, as if nothing in the world could go wrong, or come to harm any more. Steppe that was snow-covered in winter and bright green in spring, has now burnt to a pale brown. Somewhere here the artist, Joseph Beuys, crash landed his Stuka on a slushy winter's day. Then he was still a young officer, a navigator in the Luftwaffe, and was kept alive by shepherds who dragged him from the burning wreckage, smeared him with sheep's fat, and then wrapped him in felt. He was one of the heroes that Baselitz painted, one of those young soldiers inflamed with patriotic energy, cast into the hell of war and knocked speechless. The mute, huge heroes, who refused to go away and be done-over by history.

I park on the edge of the road and wander into this space that smells so fragrant and clean. Tiny white snail shells lie everywhere in the dust. Over the long ages this land has been soaked in blood countless times, but it's hard to imagine anything of this now. Ovid was banished to a place across the sea from where I am standing. He died in exile from his beloved Rome and his family estate, reflecting on his punishment but not quite coming to terms with it. Upset, lonely, cold. Certain words crop up frequently in his last works: wild, bitter, ice, snow, tears. I don't recognise his descriptions. My words are all opposite to his: hot, blue, sun-lotion, sea, salt, strawberries. Also love, happiness, peace.

In Crimea you could buy wonderful cream and meringues to go with the strawberries. I saw my first dice players, a dodgy crew on the curve of a mountain path on the way to the ruins of an old fort with their folding table, their little crowd, their small upturned tumblers that slid around so swiftly, their brazen requests to come and get robbed while everybody looked on, their aura of criminality, the fear that gathered around them. Perhaps that's what drew the punters: the kind of hypnosis a mouse experiences when it freezes under the spell of an owl's scream.

I was scared of losing money because I had never had much of it, but I was also hypnotised in a different way. The ruins drew me upwards to reach as high as I could. The steep mountain paths led to close-cropped grassy places and ledges where gulls made their homes. Far below the Black Sea looked very alive and wide, scratched with tiny waves between great circles of light. The gulls screamed as they moved off the cliffs, streaked with their lime. I lay on the edge in the wind that carried a dry-sweet smell of grasses, and wondered what it might be like to fly.

A pack of playing cards, bought this morning in Kerch lies on the passenger seat. On the front of the box is a picture of Putin in a navy beret, wearing a flying jacket undone at the neck, and a blue and white sailor's tee-shirt. He looks determined, serious, resolute. In the background are tanks, a squadron of fighter jets, a battle cruiser, and a Crimean sky touched with mackerel clouds. On the back is another picture of him in a dark suit wearing sunglasses, standing in the same gangster pose I have seen on countless tee-shirts and mugs all over Russia. The actual playing cards show snapshots of tourist spots, ruined castles, rocky crags rising from turquoise coves, dolphins jumping, the Venus de Milo perched on a new hotel roof overlooking Yalta, the lighthouse at Sevastopol. The ace of hearts has an old-styled map of the peninsula unattached to Ukraine, with a cartoon drawing of the Argo, instantly familiar with its long, low, brown-wood sides, curved prow, and oblong sail unfurled width-ways.

Ovid did not land here, but he wrote about those heroes and gods who passed by on their adventures. He had a special dread of

Medea who took the same route as Jason had taken earlier with his Argonauts, skirting the bottom of Crimea and eventually stopping at Tomis. There, in the place of Ovid's exile, in a life that was full of appalling deeds, she murdered her brother, cut his body into pieces, and scattered them in the fields except for the severed hands and head which she put in a spot where her father (who was pursuing her in his own boat) would be sure to see them. In this way she slowed her father down and made good her escape.

In the legends, her crimes undid morality and showed it to be hollow, empty, meaningless. But like currency it could be used in the pursuit of power. She felt trapped, and to free herself she rubbed morality out of the picture, not the relative morality of classes or races, but the absolute concept of good and evil, right and wrong.

I pass a big poster on the side of the road with a picture of Putin and a caption: *By 2018 the historic mission to join the Caucasus to Crimea by bridge will be completed. (signed V. Putin).* Since Kerch these posters have cropped up more or less regularly on the side of the road, each one with a different picture of Putin and a different caption: *Two new power stations are planned to be up and running during the coming year. (signed V. Putin).* Or: *Crimea and Russia will join up militarily. They will be united. (signed V. Putin)*

The sound of a jet rips through the air. I stop on the verge and look across the sky, but the noise is already hardly more than a vibration and the plane is gone. Beyond the road, the coastline has changed. The flat land between Kerch and Feodosia that met the sea in a simple horizontal strip, as in a picture by Mark Rothko, has now changed to sheer rock cliffs that rise hundreds of feet straight from the waves.

On the approach to Sudak I try to work out what I would have seen when I first arrived with Lyuba in a taxi from Simferopol twenty-five years ago, but nothing is familiar. The town still looks small, but it also looks characterless. There is no way down to the centre, the roads turn away each time, and everywhere there are construction works that have come to a stop, hotels and houses that are not quite finished, windows still missing, unused materials stacked behind steel fences.

My idea is to find the row of huts we stayed in, to knock on the sky-blue painted door, to look at the bed and the walnut tree and the washroom, to sit on the sagging mattress where we made love. I want to find the main street. There used to be a square with a bust of Lenin, old stuccoed buildings, park benches, trees for shade.

But everything has gone. Everything has been torn down. Whole sections of the town have been sectioned off. There are barriers, cabins with guards, private property signs, pedestrian-only areas. A sign on a wooden fence reads: *Enjoy yourself legally'*. I take a photo and forward it to Daisy.

I want to find the places and put everything behind me, but I can't because they're gone. The old places have been flattened and erased as if they'd never existed in the first place, and it occurs to me that the simple idea of moving on might as well be thrown-out too. It's not just the buildings and the streets which have gone, but love also. Finally it has come home: love has been demolished by life in a steady and sustained struggle for living that was impossible to fight against. It seems cruel, but I can't see a way round it.

I used to hear about Crimea from my father. It was where the English won a war, a place where the Light Brigade charged to destruction along the valley that echoed the beat of hooves as they galloped towards the cannons and death. It was also the theme of a story that settled on an old brown stretcher we once had in the house in Chalfont St Giles.

My father was knocked down by a car, in Walthamstow, on his way home from teaching in London. His hip was smashed and when he was let out of hospital they provided a stretcher for us to take home, so that we could move him around while his body healed under the plaster bandages that stretched from his stomach to his toes, with a strengthening bar between his ankles, and a hole in the back and in the front for the bedpan and the pee-bottle.

The east end of London hospital had been badly equipped, and my father used to say that he stayed alive because they didn't have the right anasthaetic, and that it was this good fortune that allowed his body time to recover during those moments when his waking agony prevented it from fading away and expiring completely.

The doctors cut up his clothes with a pair of giant scissors. Later, when he was discharged, they sent him home on the stretcher. The stretcher was heavy, with brown wood handles, and a folding iron frame that clipped open and tightened the heavy sack-like cloth. He said that the stretcher, which was extremely sturdy and of military appearance, looked as if it had been left over from the Crimean War. From then on I couldn't get this thought out of my head. The heavy camp-bed material of the stretcher was brown, the sturdy wooden handles chipped and scarred. I imagined the far off theatre of war in Crimea, the open spaces, the camps, the soldiers and the cannon balls, the blood and the guts. I imagined Florence Nightingale, and the wounded who were carried to her on this same stretcher which was so old and brown you couldn't see the blood stains anymore. Or perhaps its brown dirtiness was itself an accumulation of blood and mud from that distant war that couldn't be washed out, and had become part of the fabric of the material.

When Russia took over Crimea, in 2014, it became a subject that split friends and families. I was on the side of Russia, but only half-heartedly, and probably because I didn't understand what had really happened. Lyuba was outraged in a mild way by this support. It wasn't my country, after all, and I couldn't see the illegality and the criminal nature of the ruling ethos for what it was. In the end I was not responsible in the same way. For me it was a historical moment that I could look on with detachment. My honour was not in question.

In the old days, Lyuba used to complain of Crimea because it was where she was taken on holidays when she was young, together with her sister, and obliged to swim every day and meet with her cousins. She didn't like the sun or the swimming, or the talking with her cousins. She preferred the pioneering camps that were organised through school, those places where the children ran free in their own self-formed groups and picked fruit on the collective farms while the teachers lazed around and tried to have their own holiday.

When Lyuba first took me to Crimea it was with an almost national pride. This was what one did, what she had done, and what everyone else did, or would have liked to have done if they could have afforded it. We travelled towards the sun. First on a train, then a bus, then a taxi. But I never thought of it as famous destination, of a land that had inspired books and poems, or of a land that connected to history, despite the thoughts inspired by my father's stretcher.

We used to hang out in a bar with a blue neon sign just up the road from the beach, listening to records and drinking coffee. I remember the many hedgehogs that crossed the dusty side roads near the sea in the evenings, and the way they hurried under the wooden fences into the overgrown kitchen gardens. I remember sexy-looking women, and men who looked tough and big and brown, making their way through sunbathers in tiny bright-coloured swimming costumes. There was a party atmosphere, and we were part of it. That, in itself, was a pleasure. To be part of everyone's happiness was a new and amazing feeling.

At last I manage to get down to the sea. The promenade has been re-done. Concrete slabs separate one area off from another. It's not crowded, but there are people enjoying the sun, and everybody has the same copper-brown tan. The sea is clear and shines turquoise where the small waves foam into the dark sand.

Up on the cliff the ruined castle looks a little less ruined than it used to. The headland to the east which used to disappear into the pines is now blocked off, but in the west the steep cliff is just the same. Low rocks are visible below the water like stepping stones, and a tall, familiar-looking outcrop rises straight up from the sea like a sharp-pointed pillar.

I find a place on the beach and take my shirt and sandals off. My skin is still not really brown, though it's better than it was. Compared to the bronzed bodies all around me I look the odd one out, the pasty foreigner.

When I rest my head on the hot sand and close my eyes, spots of colour, purple and green, drift across the red darkness of my lids. The sun is heating up, working through my cells, turning me inside-out, warming up the melanocytes, drawing out their dark substance in a slow dance of life, as if everything that had ever happened, the history of the solar systems and the exploding nebulae was playing out now in a single body so that nothing might be lost.

The beginning of a story is always unclear because there are too many beginnings to choose from, and the different threads of life which form part of the same fabric pick up, one from another, without a break. At some point in the picture your own life attaches to everything else like a thread, and somewhere is its end. Not just its own end, but all those other ends that you were part of, that form the material and continue onwards and backwards.

It comes to me that amongst all these millions of beginnings and endings is a small and not-so-important end, the one I am living right now. This affair is finished. It has become clear, and the thought of these words and of what lies behind them is very real and solid, like something big that can't be talked-away anymore.

The sound of voices comes and goes over the waves. The sand smells of algae and salt and something faintly rotten. A jet ski zooms backwards and forwards, hits the swell with a bump, and disappears behind the headland. Near the rocks a windsurfer in a wetsuit, slightly obscured by his almost see-through sail, tacks across the bay.

29

'Mi scusi signore! Izvinite pozhaluysta! Per favore!'

Nothing works, even though I'm practically shouting in the man's ear. I know he's Italian by the way he answered his mobile. Then, when he began speaking Russian, the conversation became stilted and hesitant. It seems he must be deaf in one ear, the ear which is facing me, but it feels weird all the same. The waitress has seen my problem, walks over and taps him on the shoulder. Now he turns to me and for a moment I wish I'd kept quiet. He looks cross for being disturbed, on the defensive and because of his big head and big hands he also looks threatening.

I want to ask him what's happened in town, and especially what's happening beyond the wooden palings of the hotel where I am staying, where another brand-new hotel, a Disney-like hotel, has been built in the style of an Italian palazzo with rows of mock-marble columns, overhanging terracotta tiled roofs, courtyards with fountains, and a medieval bell tower with an electric chime. Perhaps he might give me a clue as to why everything looks wrong and out of place, as if a gang of saboteurs had been at work erasing the past and destroying the town at the same time. He looks like a construction manager, somebody who has been contracted in to oversee the new hotel works, the sort of person who might have information. But I'm wrong. He is Italian, but retired, and it turns out he's living here, and enjoying himself by doing nothing.

'Excuse me for interrupting your meal.' I say.

My pineapple-and-ham pizza arrives, criss-crossed all over in Thousand Island Dressing.

'This is where I come,' he gestures at the room, at the cash desk, and the sea pictures on the walls.

The waitress rearranges the paper napkins that have fallen over next to my candle.

'Ornella Muti! Some people say she's the most beautiful woman in the world. The French, they say that!'

'I was interested in one of the new hotels,' I begin.

He waits, looking at me with his fork half way to his mouth. Suddenly I can't think of what to say. In front of me is my glass of beer, the pizza which would have been okay if it wasn't smeared with so much sauce, a little candle in a glass bowl, the paper napkins newly arranged in a fan pattern. There's something challenging in his look. It's a look of rootlessness, the hard look of an adventurer, of somebody who has found a way to live where nobody will pry. It turns out that he is married to somebody from this town.

'She speaks better Italian than me. She lives in Rimini, and I'm here. All Russians pick up Italian quickly. They take to it. It comes so easily.'

I look at him, at the hairs that grow not only from inside his nostrils but also from the pock-marked skin on the outside of his nose.

'Every year I hunt. I go with my brother, with dogs, guns,' He spends a while trying to describe the animal which he hunts. Maybe it's a bird. I can't quite tell.

When I leave he stands up unexpectedly, bows, and then takes my hand in an iron-strong grip.

Back at the hotel I sit on the bed and try to figure out why I am bothered by the animal-like defences of the Italian man who talked so lovingly of Ornella Muti, the unattainable beauty. He talked of her as a connoisseur might talk of a much-admired picture, working her into the conversation and staying on the subject. At the same time his look was direct and forceful, as if he could see right through me.

Nick would say I'm making up problems, and it's true they hardly compare with the sort of human disasters he's used to reporting on. On the other hand they don't go away and their consequences are sometimes not so different. Over the years we saw enough heartache and soul-searching crises in our group of friends, and whenever something happened we were always surprised. A divorce here, a split-up there, money troubles, depression, normal selfishness, unwelcome flirtations, illness, deceit. Each time we gathered round our dinner tables with our glasses of wine and plates of food, and discussed what was to be done, our own lives and our own loves always seemed a little less secure.

At that time we all lived in south London. The mimosa which Lyuba planted in the front garden of our terraced house grew up like nobody's business. She used to joke about getting old, of being abandoned, and of what was in store for her. It was her way of keeping the problem at a distance. She saw what was coming and wanted to prepare for it, while I took the opposite view. It seemed to me that it was too soon to get worried. We were not yet old, we didn't argue or blame each other, and I couldn't see the point in flirting with unhappiness. The moment when everything went pear-shaped was the time to worry, not before.

But all the while we were losing ground. If things looked similar and felt similar, that was because we had forgotten how they used to be. What remained was a kind of uncertainty. You couldn't call it misery, it wasn't such a strong emotion. It was dull and slow.

The garden doors at the back of our house led onto a patio from where you could see the brick extensions of all the Edwardian houses on the terrace, less looked-after than they appeared from the street, with crooked windows and weeds growing out of the parapets. The backs of the houses faced south, and in the afternoon the sun would warm them up. Our extension was covered in render that had been painted at some point. The paint was worn away, and the render was cracking. In some parts it had come away from the bricks underneath. A buddleia grew up around the drain, right against the wall, and its root was forcing away a big chunk. Behind the cracked render you could see brick, and it wasn't the old yellow brick of the neighbouring houses but a new pink-coloured brick. At one time something must have gone wrong with this wall and it had been rebuilt and rendered and repainted. Still, it looked solid.

Immovable. Ugly. Hard. Obdurate. It towered over our patio as a reminder of the difficulty of ever changing, and of trying to make something different. We waited, while all around our friends' problems took on the proportions of tragedy. We watched as their lives unravelled on the streets of Tulse Hill and East Dulwich as in an opera with grand gestures, weeping heroines and villains.

Years ago I drove with Nikolai through the country near Tambov, on the way back from his bee farm, and pointed out a burning house to him. It was an old log house with a fenced in garden set in an open field. Twenty foot flames poured through the roof and windows. We didn't stop, and afterwards I recited the ladybird song in Russian: 'Ladybird, Ladybird, fly away home, your house is on fire and your children are gone!'

For him, the end of an era had coincided with the emigration of his daughter, and the end of his own working life. Many of his friends had already left Russia, and while it seemed in the beginning that cruelty lay in the impossibility of return, it turned out that the opposite was true. Old travel restrictions were the cause of real suffering when members of the same family found themselves cut off from each other, but they also concentrated love and devotion. A trapped life was strangely cosy and meaningful after all, and it turned out that the bitter taste of indifference was worse than the grief of separation. The big story was finished, and there was nothing to fight for anymore.

I came to enjoy those times in summer when Lyuba took the children to Russia and I stayed on at home. Everybody got some breathing space, and sometimes I followed them out for a week or a fortnight, and sometimes not. There was always work to get on with. Usually the children left their school early, before the school holidays had officially begun. Daisy's friends in Russia, Masha and Tanya, would already be in Vashutino. It was a great thing, the long Russian holiday that continued from June to September. And after they left, when I saw the local primary school kids trooping to school with their bags in the mornings for another three weeks, I felt bad for them all, especially when the days were hot. There was a special energy that gathered in London early in the morning, when the day was going to be sweltering. The sun summoned its strength when it was still only just clear of the roofs and chimney pots, as if preparing to concentrate its rays for the midday onslaught. Traffic began building up on the road leading to the junction at Herne Hill. Kids cut through the park. Parents followed the kids. Whole families trooped across the grass with their buggies and their dogs.

Sometimes I got a call from Vashutino, sometimes not. Leila, our eldest daughter, who was born just a few weeks after our wedding, was working in Luxembourg. Boris had a job in London. He visited from time to time with his girlfriend, and was tall now, much taller than me, with long hair and a big beard. I was used to him as an adult, and I still remembered him very well as a child, but somehow the whole middle period of his life seemed to have been wiped clean. I couldn't connect the two people together, the big man and the little boy. And it was the same with myself. I was used to my reflection staring back at me when I shaved in the morning, but it didn't connect in any way to my early life. It wasn't just that I now had grey hairs, or that an up-close examination revealed greasy patches on the skin, bits of dandruff, and networks of broken blood vessels running across the whites of my eyes into the corners. Sometimes I was simply confused. I couldn't work out who was staring back at me, and what this man was doing there in my bathroom.

I still looked forward to Lyuba and the younger kids returning, and would get the house cleaned up and something cooked to eat. On the day of the flight I would try to look nice. I would arrive at Heathrow with plenty of time to spare, and stand behind the barriers in Terminal Two next to the coffee shop, looking at all the people as they came through. The flight from Moscow was easy to spot. There was something extra-businesslike about the Russians who travelled alone. The families glided past as units, all of a kind. And then there were always one or two of the old Soviet intellectual types, their heavy-thinking foreheads creased in craggy, characterful lines.

The children would run to meet me, suntanned, bigger, stumbling with their English. Usually Lyuba had managed to dye her hair back to its old colour. Sometimes she did it too dark, and it came out looking strange, like a wig. She was always tanned too, though it didn't suit her so much.

At home the bags were unzipped on the living room floor, and for a moment there was a pause as those last instructions or promises or responsibilities were remembered. And then everything was unwrapped, bags of Russian sweets, pieces of home-cured fish, honey from Nikolai's friend's farm, bottles of vodka, black bread, caviar.

After everything edible had been dumped on the kitchen table the children would go to their rooms and their computers and phones, and Lyuba would make herself a cup of tea. She would get out her laptop and run through photos. I would open one of Nikolai's bottles, and for the time being everything was okay. Neither of us wanted trouble or wanted to go backwards, but there was nothing we could do. It was as if life was determined to have its own way and swamp us. Soon everything was back to the same old difficulties, the same sense that things were going to run their course until we were both incapable of doing anything different.

It was a dull problem, and from Lyuba's point of view simple. If I couldn't get on with how things were, I could leave. There was nothing stopping me. Neither of us was particularly weak. If one of us walked out, the other would survive. I understood that leaving was the sensible thing to do, on the other hand it was also inconceivable and horrifying, the sort of thought that would occur to a drunken house-wrecker. I was in a position of someone who tries to face an issue head-on and doesn't realise that the problem is not just in front of them, but all around them, and rising up inside them.

30

The train runs north, through the flatlands on the edge of Ukraine. Lines of poplars move across each other at different speeds, the closer ones moving more quickly than the further trees, as if they had been separate voices in a grand fugue.

I'm sharing the carriage with two train drivers. They smile across at me, and we say hello. Soon I'm listening to their bawdy stories. Perhaps this is a special train driver's style, a closed union in which you are protected and where you may say what you like among comrades. They talk of fucking this or that woman, as if they had been describing the preparations butchers make with their slabs of fresh meat. They look at me and smile, laugh at each other's stories, slap their knees, and get themselves going again with the thought of knocking up one or other of the station mistresses.

And they are enthusiastic about the trains too. They talk of the power of the engines and of how the pistons pump. (Here they spread their legs apart, push their hips forward and, with hands outstretched as if grasping something really substantial, begin to thrust their bottoms up and down). A few minutes before the stop where they will sleep before taking a shift, they take out memorabilia from their wallets – pictures of German officers dressed in Nazi regalia. One of them, the one with the slightly redder, pointier nose, shows me a picture of himself holding what looks to be an SS belt with a swastika on the buckle. This is his token of friendship. He has let me into his world.

We are passing the edge of a plain that stretches for more than a thousand miles westwards, fields of black earth that once provided enormous surpluses of wheat, the same lands that fell victim to central planning as hunger shaped the destiny of populations. Not far away are the places where watchtowers with armed men were set up to arrest those who entered the fields searching for food during the famines, while the bodies of the starved were piling up outside the villages. It's evening and we pull into a station. Everybody gets up from their seats to get some air, and the guards step outside and wait by the open doors with their flags.

The village station is quiet. People walk up and down the platform and chat in front of the station house where there is a queue for meat pasties. A man and his son carry a string of smoked fish for sale. Their skin is as brown as the fish they carry, and their long bare backs are almost identical, like two smoothly shaped Russian dolls. When they turn they both smile in the same way too, though the man laughs with flashes of gold and gaps; a rough, not particularly kindly face.

The following morning we reach the first of the market gardens outside Moscow. Dark wood houses give way to high-rise apartments. There are more roads, we pass a road with a traffic jam, then a river winding round a wooded slope, more tower blocks, domed churches caught between high-rises, more people in the streets, more cars, warehouses, railway hoardings, old engines, strings of empty carriages, station huts and signal boxes, sidings, and towards the end a whole army of rusty rails joining the main tracks until there are too many rails to count.

For a while as we run alongside the platform it's stop-start, as if there was something wrong with the brakes. We slow down, and then start rolling backwards. The train judders, squeaks, stops, and then moves smoothly forwards again. Finally we come to a stop for the last time, right on schedule.

Moscow was always a city of dreams, the town of a thousand domes, of glamour and squalor, of beautiful fur hats and red star generals, of May Day parades and erratic policies. It was always the most hated and most loved city, a place of peeling stucco palaces and of stragglers arriving from somewhere else and hoping to make it for a while. It was the place where people came from all over to study and from where, in the old days, the newly qualified doctors, engineers, and specialists of all kinds were sent out on work placements across the empire. It's where they met and the place they dreamed of when they were old and tired and eking out their lives in the provinces. It was always a city on the make and a town that had seen it all before, a hard place and a place of fairy-tale presumption with an architecture like nowhere else. It was the place where everybody always wanted to be.

I was out walking one winter evening towards midnight and came across a woman lying unconscious, flat in the snow. I tried to move her, to lift her off the ground, but she was too heavy. She had a puffy face and pink lipstick. A warm smell of perfume and beer rose off her body. I went to get help and was told to forget it, that someone would be coming to claim her. The next morning I passed by the same place, and she had gone. I felt a stab of regret that I hadn't returned, that I had listened to that person who had told me to forget it.

Now I make my way slowly through Paveletsky vokzal and out on the street, where I take the metro to the zoo. I don't want to miss anything this time round. Maybe it's foolish to resurrect the past – and not so interesting. Sometimes it's sad, too, but only a little. The past is already too far-off to be very affecting, too small, too insignificant. And yet there's no harm in thinking of it.

Some memories float to the surface after a long time, and then stay in view and don't go away. And sometimes an experience seems permanent from the start, right from when you first have it. Something mundane or catchy will detach itself from everyday life, and at that moment you know it will not go away, and that you will always remember it.

Many years ago when I was out walking, I found myself on a tree lined street in an area of town I didn't know well. It was warm and peaceful, and for a moment it seemed to me that I had discovered a magic place, a kind of paradise. A few minutes later I heard shouting coming from one of the rooms on the upper floor of an apartment block. The windows were open and the screaming was violent, as if the two people inside were ripping each other to pieces. There was a crash and the sound of breaking glass, and a large alarm clock came flying through the window. It bounced on the road in front of me with a smaller burst of shattered glass, and a few seconds later the bell went off and the clock began to twist awkwardly across the road on its unwinding key. I watched it move into the gutter and run out. Up in the tenement the screaming had stopped.

Here the roads are busy, crammed with cars. Many of the places are hard to recognise. There is a kiosk near to the subway by the zoo. There are shops where there used to be institutions. I begin to mark out my memories, trying to get my bearings, and it seems to me that it was exactly here, twenty-five years ago, that I was sniffed by a giant rat. I was on my way to Aviamotornaya for dinner. It was a summer evening and I was waiting, thinking, in a dream about something or other. I noticed a man in a camel-hair coat pointing at my shoes. I looked down and there it was, a large, grey thing, biting the hem of my trousers. I shook my leg and the rat scurried off under some bins. I thought: Why me?

I walk up the street to the square that commemorates the 1905 uprising. The metro station was shot up in 1993. Now it looks different and shinier than I remember. There are large, ever-evolving neon signs, and lots of new buildings. I don't recognise much at all on Presnensky Val. The street looks bigger, and more open. The classic Moscow tenement where Lyuba lived has gone. Instead there is a new brown building with glass balconies.

Two shipping containers have been put on top of each other near the entrance of the zoo, to make a restaurant. Fire-escape steps lead upwards to the front door, and inside it's stylish and warm with large windows overlooking the park. A group of flamingos stands watch under the birches near to a large plastic whale that is raised off the ground with a door let into the side. Some older teenagers are putting coins into the slot and then watching while it goes through its diving and rolling sequence. Probably they stole the money from somebody's grandmother. Apart from this little gang the place is quiet. There are no children watching the animals, no parents with pushchairs, just this disreputable group, and the flamingos standing guard.

I order carp and a carafe of vodka. The last time I was in Moscow I met Leonid's daughter, Maya. We went for a drink and she let me know how the atmosphere was becoming unbearable in the country, how television was constantly whipping up ludicrous enmities, and how normal social freedoms were being squeezed by morons. She was thinking of leaving Russia altogether and joining her father in Germany. Everybody seemed to be leaving Russia, though for different reasons. Berezovsky was still alive then, living in England. 'Write him a letter asking him to pay the fines of all those people who have been threatened not to protest!' Maya said. Now Berezovsky has gone, found hanging from a shower rail in his bathroom, leaving no note, no explanation.

For fifteen years a wave of Russian money crashed westwards and streamed through London, Paris, Frankfurt. The foam floated off the top and settled in Surrey, Kensington, the Riviera, Venice. Though perhaps less in Venice. There is a cemetery in Venice with a Russian corner where Stravinsky and Brodsky and Diaghilev are buried, but that's not such a draw; you cannot, after all, drive a car in Venice, and these people are interested in cars. Cars and helicopters. Planes. Security. Secret recording apparatus. Large leather armchairs, and big shiny desks. Metal gates. Fences with cameras, and unsmiling bodyguards.

These particular Russians always stick together, taking over quiet squares in the chic centres of town. They also have a particular liking for fake Edwardian mansions in the suburbs with plenty of garage space and near to golf courses - though they don't play golf. They cause mild outrage, then boredom. They keep to themselves, and unless you go looking for them you will not see them except, perhaps, through the thick glass of high-end Japanese restaurants.

I remember a man called Grisha. His wife was involved with cultural events in the Russian community, and there was a time when we used to see each other at parties in London. He had been on the board of Yukos, the giant oil conglomerate, before its assets were seized by the state. An economics student at Moscow State University, a pal of Khodorkovsky, he was banished from Russia and will probably go to jail if he returns. He lives in Weybridge, in Surrey, not far from Berezovsky's old home. He always gave the impression of a real thug, cunning, boorish, a person you would instinctively turn away from in public, too full of himself, arrogant and without style. A show-off, and perhaps not even particularly intelligent, though he had a special kind of honesty, not of honour but of effectiveness. You got the feeling that if he meant to get something done he most probably would. He was a dynamo around which a whole crowd of hangers-on hoped to get a foothold. His money, or rather the promise of his money (nobody knew just how much he was worth), was enough to turn otherwise sensible people off their heads. Anybody who came into his orbit was instantly sucked in, whether they liked it or not. The thought of such wealth made havoc, like a great wind passing through. Nobody was safe. It cut a swathe through relationships, through organisations, through government departments. It put everybody off their balance, and it was a great relief to everyone when it had passed.

So what should I write to Berezovsky? Too late to ask for money. What do I want to know? How he died? Why he died?

A waiter brings chilled vodka with a basket of salt-glazed bread. I pour off a small glass, tear off some bread, and think: What has changed? Or rather, what is holding things together? What does it take to see things differently?

In the spring of 1987, an eighteen-year-old German called Mathias Rust made a calculation. He decided that with favourable weather conditions and with extra fuel tanks he would be able to charter a plane and, without telling anyone of this plan, fly from Helsinki over the Gulf of Finland and cross into Estonia. He would then make his way south to Latvia, keeping clear of the larger towns, cut due east over the border into Russia and fly in a straight line over all the hundreds of lakes and miles of pine forests until he reached Moscow. This was all forbidden territory, guarded night and day by a fearsome hi-tech army, a military bristling with enough heavy weaponry to wipe out the whole world. Even now, it's hard for me to imagine somebody with the kind of reckless bravery needed to do this, to ignore an empire that prided itself on its virility and its ability to crush an enemy.

He prepared with a minimum of fuss, removing three passenger seats from a hired plane and fitting extra fuel tanks in their place. His first cross-water flight took him from Denmark over the North

Sea to the Shetland Isles, where he refuelled and stayed overnight. From the Shetland Isles he made his way further north to the Faroe Isles and then on another five hundred miles to Iceland. There, he hung around the community hall in Reykjavik near to the harbourside. Not very far away was the French embassy building where Gorbachev and Reagan had recently met, and failed to come to an agreement on arms reductions. Reagan had made a big deal out of the new defensive shield technology that used lasers, mirrors stationed in space, and electric guns. Billions of dollars were already pumping into programs designed to knock out any enemy missile before it reached its target. In the meantime the Soviet budget was in trouble and running dry. Everything had already been spent.

The following day Rust flew to Bergen, stayed the night in a hotel, and then carried on to Helsinki. Helsinki lies opposite Tallinn, and at this point the Gulf of Finland narrows down to about sixty miles, or around half an hour in a small plane. The following day he took off on the last leg of his journey. Once he had reached his cruising altitude over the water he settled on a steady course west by southwest. Air traffic control in Helsinki had Stockholm down as his route, so when he made an about-turn and headed south east, turning his radio equipment off, they assumed mechanical failure. And yet nobody, neither the Finns nor the Russians, seemed to worry much about Rust that day. A Finnish search and rescue party gave up looking, deciding that he had plummeted into the sea and disappeared forever. The Russians did see him and two MiGs were scrambled, came up close and tracked him for a minute or so. Then, having been told not to worry themselves over this oddity, they swung away and were gone.

All the way over Estonia and Latvia, across Belarus and on to Moscow, he was ignored. Whenever his plane was picked up on radar the sector responsible allotted it a friendly code, a helper in an accident, a passing helicopter – just whatever was most convenient to dismiss it.

Rust landed on a bridge below the Kremlin and taxied up the slope to Red Square, coming to a stop in front of St Basil's Cathedral. He was quickly surrounded by a crowd. Then the police arrived in a van. The Cessna was towed away for inspection, and Rust was driven straight to Lefortovo jail.

Zinik kept a photo of Rust's landing in the hallway of his flat, next to a pair of small American flags of the sort you push into birthday cakes. Whenever I saw the picture of the plane on the cobbles of the square, with Rust still seated inside, I would think of those magicians or escape artists who took their art to the next level, into the realms of the sublime, almost by accident.

...

The teenagers have abandoned the painted whale. My waiter has already checked if I really do want the carp. It's all bones he says. In England, carp is said to have a muddy taste. But it turns out that the muddy taste is what some people like about it. In England, if you order chicken feet in a Chinese restaurant they will ask the same question: 'Are you sure?' The same goes for a story – it can be told one way or another. Maybe you won't like it, or maybe you will. Maybe you are supposed to dislike it, but there is something about it that appeals to you.

Berezovsky started out life as a Jew. Then he turned to the Orthodox church. I was taken to church when I was small and presumed that everybody thought as I did, that all the promises and vows were nothing more than words. I didn't go further and ask why the congregation needed to repeat them every week, and perhaps my rebellion had something personal in it. Perhaps I really didn't belong there.

Lyuba's mother was born into an old Jewish family. Like other Jews in Russia she had her internal passport stamped *Jew*. Like other Jews all over the world she was the butt of playground taunts, but the taunting was rare, there were certain moments only, and when she was adult she said that, in the end, it hadn't really bothered her. She looked back and made a story of it when she was trying to make sense of her life. She married Nikolai, a non-Jew, and that was that. They lived in a nice flat left to them by her parents who had been well-off, educated people. There were books, pictures, a piano. Her father had been an officer in Berlin when it had fallen, and had brought back the beautiful old china clock which was put in pride of place on the mantelpiece in the front room of their flat that overlooked the Lefortovo jail. They kept their skis in the toilet, and a racing bike on the outside balcony.

Nikolai worked in the military as an electrical engineer on the advance warning systems for detecting incoming missiles. Olga worked as a researcher in a computer factory. They took holidays apart because it was cheaper that way. They saved up and Olga took the children to Crimea in summer, staying in the small town of Sudak on the Black Sea while Nikolai worked.

Olga was always enthusiastic about something or other. She was one of those who are susceptible to crazes, special things to eat, novel ways of curing illness. She became addicted to Yoga, then Christianity. When she was forty-eight she met two proselytising Mormons and converted to Mormonism. Nikolai followed in her footsteps dutifully. They held hands and immersed themselves in a bathing pool wearing white, sheet-like costumes.

Her embrace of new things is extreme, and it doesn't matter so much what it is she connects herself to. Not so long ago she gave up on Mormonism and discovered her Jewishness again. Now she encourages the children. They sit around the table in her flat when they are back from Vashutino and on the way to London. The china clock brought back from the ruins of Germany has gone, but otherwise not much has changed. They sing songs for Sabbath, light candles, clasp their hands together, and do a little dance. The last time this happened Miles was less willing to get into the spirit of things. 'If you aren't going to sing properly we can stop altogether,' Olga threatened him. He looked at her uncertainly, trying to read her meaning. Slowly he lifted his hands from his lap and placed them on the edge of the tablecloth, ready to begin the clapping and sing the song. Daisy looked over the table, anxious for her Grandmother to begin. And so it started up again, three childish voices rising up and down excitedly, as if they were all very happy.

...

It isn't enough to see coincidences, to note them as they stack up. Somehow they have to make sense, or else be understood. Not so long ago I found out that my mother had begun learning Russian when she was pregnant with me. She started in a compulsive, irrational way, and continued through until I was born, when she gave up and didn't give it another thought. There was no reason for her to learn Russian, she had no plans to travel there, no Russian friends or relatives. And now I think to myself that if I was to tell this story in the way it should be told – this particularly Russian story – it should start here, at the very beginning, in my mother's womb, and with the impulse of life's first move.

I always wanted consistency and truth, or whatever it was that corresponded most closely to how I saw things. It was difficult, because like many people I lived as if I was solving a problem, and thought in a way that made it hard to see other points of view. When we moved out of my parent's house and back to London again, I forgot all I had ever learned and dreamed of, and gave up everything to bring in money. In the evenings I was often too tired even to read. Year after year it was the same, though I always thought of what was going to happen next, and of how things were going to be once everything was sorted.

In the end the children got on with their own lives, and hardly noticed when I wasn't around. The decision to leave was a private one, not talked of, and something of a non-event. I called on the telephone often, and saw everybody at weekends. The house I moved to was far from everything, but it was close to Harwich, and I wanted to be there, on the North Sea coast near to where the boat leaves for Zeebrugge. This was the old route to Russia, the way back that started with a train from Liverpool Street, the same route Lyuba used the first time she returned home. The big windows faced east, towards Russia, and when the sun came up over the fields it flooded the rooms with dull orange light.

I often drove to the sea, though I only ever managed to arrive when it was almost dark. A blue boat was pulled up on the shingle. The lights of a wind farm glowed faintly down the coast, and those thoughts of my old life were mixed up with the damp stones and the sound of water, and the screams of seagulls that gathered on a rig that stood in the shallow water not far from the shore.

Once I left the house earlier and drove further down the coast to a place where the river cuts through the lowlands. There was a harbour with muddy banks and a dyke. Beyond the river was a large and featureless spit of land. Children dangled lines into the water from a wooden bridge, and every once in a while they pulled them out and shook translucent crabs the size of a fingernail into their catch-buckets.

I used a ferry service, and crossed over to the opposite bank in a small open boat. Then I took a path towards the strip of sea in the distance. At first the path ran along the edge of a marsh, but soon the grass fell away and, for as far as you could see, the land was covered in shingle. There were patches of blue kale and, to the north, the masts of a Cold War radar station. The station had been raised with American money. Now it was abandoned. The era of the Cold War was over. The war had died, together with its props, its spy ships posing as rusty trawlers, its huge missile projects, its assassinations, its bluff and incompetence.

It was heavy walking on the shingle. A lighthouse stood by the sea, right on the edge of the spit. The tide was high and the waves were small, and lapped up the shingle slope without energy. Further on, blast-testing buildings and abandoned bunkers dripped with slime. Slabs of concrete lay sideways, riddled with bomb blast test holes. Heavy iron rails, unmovable without a crane, slowly rusted away.

There was a cruelty to everyday life that I rebelled against. I went to sleep at odd times during the day and woke up on the sofa downstairs, uncertain where I was. The family dog, now my dog, followed me everywhere as if trying to help. It seemed she knew things, and that this knowledge was bound up with an intuition that we would never be able to fully communicate. One day she began sniffing in a tangle of irises that grew thickly all around the pond, her tail quivering with excitement. She jerked her head twice, and then turned with a baby moorhen hanging limply from her mouth, one of a small family I had been watching over the past weeks from the kitchen window.

I re-read Shalamov. I was looking for the story set in Kolyma after his release from the prison camp system. In the story he receives news of a telegram that is waiting for him. He's full of dread because a telegram can mean only one thing - death. But at the postal office, behind the three barbed wire fences, the abandoned chicken houses, and the wandering pigs he is told that the telegram says simply that a letter is waiting for him. The depot where the letters arrive from Moscow is five hundred kilometres away, in Magadan. He does not have a coat and nor does he know who the letter is from, but he decides in the end to go anyway. He buys a coat from an old crook, with the bottom part cut away, and sets off through the snow. Grey, exhausted, still ill, wearing the mutilated coat that is not warm enough, he hitches a lift across the northern wastes at a ruble-a-kilometre from a lorry driver who drinks a super-strength brew of black tea to keep himself awake, a whole tin of leaves boiled in a can of water and then left to cool in the snow.

When Shalamov finally arrives at the depot, frozen through and almost dead after making his way across town, it turns out that the letter addressed to him, and still preserved as if by a miracle, is from Pasternak.

I used to make tea as I was first given it on the Paris-Moscow train. Then it was served in a tall glass that fitted in a silver holder with a curved handle, so you could see the clear gold-brown colour. I put sugar in, and a piece of lemon. But since reading that story by Shalamov I began to do it differently. For a long time now, I have made it very strong and stewed, in a big cup without sugar or lemon or milk, and I think of the lorry driver in Kolyma, and of the chifir that kept him awake.

A picture hung on the wall at the top of the stairs of the house in Suffolk that I couldn't help seeing every night when I went to bed. It was an old double portrait left by David, the ex-owner of the house, who had asked me to keep it for a while before he found time to dispose of it. The old varnish and heavily ornamented frame reminded me of a picture in my family home in Chalfont St Giles, the sunset epic called *The Return of the Herd* by Farquharson. A photocopied paper was stuck behind the frame, and one day I pulled it out and found that the portrait was of a man called Charles Whitworth, an ambassador in St Petersburg at the time of Peter the Great. The figure on the right of the picture was his nephew. The photocopied entry also explained that after Whitworth's death a piece of writing had been rescued from his official correspondence and published, and that this book (all about Russia) had been an instant hit and had remained on the bestselling list for thirty years.

I felt like laughing out loud. It seemed preposterous as well as unbelievable, but it was all quite true. The picture faced me every night on my way to bed and also in the morning when it was bathed in the soft glow of the rising sun. I passed it on the way to the toilet, and it was so big that I couldn't help noticing it whenever I opened the front door or crossed the entrance hall. Both sitters, old and young, wore white wigs, and both stared out in the same direct way. The eyes of the younger one, especially, seemed to bore straight through me with an overwhelming righteous power. I wrote to David, who lived up in Scotland, telling him I really didn't want it, that this enormous picture was giving me the creeps, but I got no reply.

31

After Napoleon's defeat at Waterloo, England and Russia both celebrated by building churches. In London five churches were built in the classic Palladian style, in West Norwood, Brixton, Camden, Oval and Waterloo - just down from the bridge, where the rough-sleepers shelter and where they are given soup once a day.

Russia decided on one big church and then forgot to build it. The Tsar (Alexander I) died. But then his son, Nicholas I, began to dwell on the plans. Nicholas disliked the original classical designs which had been forgotten about (and which were similar in style to those white stone churches with greek, temple-like columns in London). Instead he proposed a domed church. And so work began on what was to be the biggest orthodox cathedral in the world, with no expense spared. The walls were six feet thick, the inside was decorated with Italian marble, inlaid with precious stones and frescoed. The domes were waterproofed with sheets of gold.

Nicholas died before it was completed. Then his son oversaw the ceremony of consecration which was also the occasion of the premier of Tchaikovsky's 1812 Overture with cannon. Then he died too. Prokudin Gorsky took a photo of the church from the Kremlin walls and included it in his mega collection of Russian life. And that was that. But then something quite unexpected happened: in 1931 Stalin ordered the building to be blown up.

Carved into the walls of this quite-new exceedingly well built and lavish church were the names of the thousands who had fallen while defending the motherland against the French. The thought of blowing up this memorial didn't pose a problem to Stalin. It didn't matter so much about the people who had died defending Russia. What mattered was the creation of something stupendous and better, a general enterprise headed up by god-like figures, immortals carved in stone, cast in bronze, remembered by cities.

Simultaneously, as the building was dynamited, the Moscow planning committee announced a competition. Architects the world over were invited to submit plans for a new building. The competition sparked major excitement, and while the demolition of the cathedral was looked on with horror, the thought of becoming involved in what was to come set the architects' studios buzzing. Everybody entered plans who could afford to. In the end the city's chief architect decided on a truly extraordinary design, a futuristic temple, outsized, beyond human scale, and topped by a colossal bronze of Lenin so big that it would be seen thirty miles away. It was to be a monument to World Communism, in Communism's capital. The world's most grandiose building topped by the world's biggest statue.

But just as the cathedral building was delayed following Napoleon's defeat, so this building was delayed too. Materials were appropriated for the war effort. Water seeped into the foundation pits and remained there, stagnating. Bushes sprouted everywhere. It became a derelict wasteland, a favourite spot for down-and-outs, a hiding place for crooks, a place for prostitutes to work. It was fenced off, but that didn't stop people. Holes were made in the fence, wire was cut, planks pried apart. Kids played in the ruins. The extraordinary building that was to be a palace to the Soviets was forgotten about.

Then, in the 1950's, an open-air swimming pool was built on the site, the biggest open air swimming pool in the world. It was heated and steamed in the winter like a Turkish bath. It was a beautiful dream, a fantasy where with your body already immersed pleasantly in warm water you pushed through soft polythene strips into the bright, cold air.

Ryszard Kapuscinski wrote about this swimming pool in his book on Russia, a funny episode in a book with many funny episodes. But his story stops short of the most bizarre ending to this most famous of outdoor pools. Following a request from the Holy Synod of Moscow, in 1994, the most beautiful swimming pool in the world was drained and bulldozed, scraped up, heaped into piles, loaded into lorries and taken away. Now an exact replica of the old-new church of Christ the Saviour stands on the same site once more. Again, extraordinary amounts of money have been lavished on its construction. A service was held, elevating the last Tsar's family to sainthood. Yeltsin lay there for a few days before being taken to Novodevichy Cemetery. Soon afterwards the punk rock group Pussy Riot set themselves up inside and sang a song to the Virgin Mary, urging Putin to go and fuck himself.

East goes west. The great migrations of the world follow the sun. Russia always looked westwards from its position of relative eastness. But when the new socialist state was being manufactured it closed itself off. The new empire was enclosed within a zillion miles of barbed wire. It was equipped with buffer zones of influence bursting with vigorous hatred. Only few things were allowed out. Natural resources were allowed out. Sports teams were allowed out. I remember looking at pictures of a Moskvitch car around the breakfast table in Chorleywood. It wasn't streamlined but it was durable looking and extremely shiny. My father said: 'It'll be good to start in cold weather'.

Fear was let out, often cynically and dramatically, but sometimes inadvertently. A select group of people managed to jump ship. You had a chance if you were already travelling abroad. Sports stars defected suddenly. Army officers defected suddenly. Famous musicians ran away. Piatigorsky escaped by jumping onto a train at the border as it was leaving and survived - though his cello was shot to pieces by a guard. Rostropovich landed at Heathrow airport with his two enormous white poodles and declared his undying love for Russia. He was allowed to bring in his cello, but the dogs were locked up. Now he's lying in Novodevichy Cemetery too, not very far from Yeltsin.

Sometimes escape was spectacular. A keen swimmer and oceanographer jumped ship quite literally. In the fifties the Soviet government ran a cruise operation from the port of Vladivostok. It took tourists south, towards the south seas and the beauty of those sun-drenched islands. But being Soviet it couldn't actually stop in any of them. It couldn't even go very close. As a paying passenger you had to be content with sailing in the general direction and dressing up in straw hats and sunglasses *as if* you were partying on the beach. Slava Kurilov smuggled a pair of flippers into his cabin and jumped in the night. He swam for two days before crawling half-dead onto a sandy beach in the Philippines (where he was put in jail).

People slipped through the cracks. In many ways the so-called Iron Curtain was more like a sluice gate, or like a whole line of sluice gates, damp, tall, encrusted in weed, dripping and creaking under the pressure. Even when they were shut they were not completely water-tight. And the sluice gates that were shut for fifty years defined the history of Russia. Nobody is in agreement about what it might have been like before the sluice gates were built, but everyone seems quite certain of what life was like in relation to the sluice gates, and in relation to freedom. There is a picture of Solzhenitsyn in Vermont after his emigration. He has his trademark sparse beard, lines of suffering run down his face, or maybe they're lines that have developed because he's old and his muscles have softened. He throws his head back and shuts his eyes. He exclaims: 'Freedom! This is what Freedom smells like! At last!' Nobody would dream of contradicting him, but where did he first get this taste of freedom to know what it really smelt like?

The waiter brings the carp with a certain degree of ceremony in this smart restaurant in which I am the only diner. The gold-grey skin is decorated with slivers of red pepper, roasted so that the edges are just turning black. The fish's face has lost its greedy expression and looks more like a scraped and faded painting on an old plate. I pull it apart gently and take a piece in my mouth, feeling with my tongue for any stray needle-thin bones.

I have some old photographs taken from Olga and Nikolai's flat, and I spread them on the starched tablecloth. They are black and white prints which I developed myself and some of the exposure is uneven, some have not been fixed well and have faded, and some curl up at the edges. They're all familiar: Lyuba and me sitting in an abandoned bath in the middle of a Moscow street, Lyuba kneeling in front of a glass cabinet in her flat with Boris in her arms, me on the beach in Crimea, a gold chain around my neck, small nylon trunks, my face lost in a glare of sunlight.

I don't feel so old but it's clear to me that I must be. In the photos I look different, slim, almost slight. I can't remember feeling different, but the photos don't show what I feel. Some of the photos I remember only as photos, and the actual moments are more difficult to conjure up.

I pick out one, a familiar one which I never liked very much of Lyuba with our friend, Inyutin, before he made his money and bought his factory. It has been taken in Bolshevo, at the old dacha which used to belong to Olga's family. Inyutin is reaching over and holding onto Lyuba's nose. He has a piece of barbecued chicken in one hand. It all looks too bright, Inyutin looks like a monkey, Lyuba's eyes are shut, her face scrunched up, and there is a grease stain on the blanket. Or perhaps the dark mark has something to do with the way the print has been washed, a spot of undiluted acid maybe. I don't remember taking this picture but I remember the occasion very well. We were sitting around in the upstairs room waiting for somebody to arrive, a friend of Inyutin's and Lyuba's, called Sasha. Sasha was something of a womaniser, attractive, popular. Everybody liked him, I liked him, Lyuba liked him. Apparently his mother doted on him and he was an obedient son. And now he was late for the barbecue and we were sitting around eating too much chicken, getting greasy faces and hands. I was a little jealous of Sasha, there's no denying it. He had known Lyuba for longer than I had. She used to be crazy about him when she was still in school, but for some reason he resisted her. Then Lyuba married Boris's father and put him out of her mind. After that Sasha became more attentive and this time Lyuba resisted him.

When I first arrived this on-off unconsummated affair was off again, and I didn't make an issue of it. It would have been surprising if there hadn't been admirers and lovers, somewhere or other in the background. Lyuba really was beautiful and had always attracted attention, but I can only remember one time, on the way back from Bolshevo to Moscow on the train, when I questioned her on the subject. Lyuba told me that she hated jealous men and so I managed to change, to put those thoughts out of my head. And in fact there really was nothing to worry about. We were both happy with each other. We didn't need other people, though we both had an idea of how this might change, and this intuition made us sad, as if we could see the end, something inevitable that cannot be fought against, that vague future which I am living now.

The buildings I stayed in are no longer standing. The flat where Lyuba knelt in front of the glass cabinet has been bulldozed. I have been to that dacha in Bolshevo where we waited for Sasha and got greasy hands. It took a while to understand what had happened. A concrete wall with art-deco style decorative panelling that used to follow the gardens all the way down to the station is still standing. There is a small square of grass with a tree that used to belong to the orchard next to the house. Otherwise this old and genteel district of lindens, wide pathways, and generously proportioned wooden houses is all gone. Even the space near to the station where the market was, and where the beer truck used to pull up, is gone. You cannot see the train tracks anymore. Apartment blocks, twenty five stories high, have sprung up everywhere. A motorway runs where the old road used to be, a concrete flyover with slip roads that curl round and down, inaccessible and always busy.

•••

When I first arrived in Moscow I was told by Lyuba that if I said one good word about Gorbachev she would stop sleeping with me. It wasn't such a tough decision. I thought for a moment of my own convictions: what were they? I couldn't kid myself that I had any, and when I asked her what she didn't like about him she didn't answer. Finally, she said that it was his voice, that it was unpleasant, provincial, heavy with mis-pronunciations. This made sense to me, and if I didn't have those convictions which might have provided me with a means to judge things, I did have an enormous appetite for looking, for wandering around and taking everything in.

I had a camera and I spent my time taking pictures and developing them. I took cine film and developed that too. The colour rolls were draped around the flat to dry, like streams of burnt Christmas decorations. I got to know the city on foot. Sometimes I cycled. I used to go long distances on the bike, taking roads out of town. I took the metro a lot. There was a stop just up the road from Olga and Nikolai's flat at a big junction where super-sized pipes crossed over the street and tall chimneys smoked all day and night, their red and white striped columns with brick corbelling showing the date of construction - 1974. There weren't so many cars. There were small Zhigulis modelled on the Fiats of the sixties, and Volgas, most of them taxis, which were larger and more American-styled. The trucks were always rotten old hulks in terrible condition, and you could hear that they were on their last legs. When I took the bike I was the only cyclist on the roads.

One day the streets were completely quiet. There was no traffic, though people were out. Oldsters walked with their medals pinned proudly to their jackets, veterans decked out in their once-a-year outfits. They hung around street corners and by the kiosks, enjoying the moment. It was the annual May Day parade, the day in Moscow's calendar when all you needed to do was get up early and, who knows, you might even get a glimpse of the leader, a moment that for many people caught in their minds and stayed with them forever. Every year the same miracle was presented, the same spectacular with gymnasts, musicians, children's parades, 'The People' carrying banners and red flags, the slow progress of outsized portraits of heroes of the Revolution, soldiers, weapons. Huge missiles were dragged past the generals on multi-wheeled flatbed carriers. Smaller missiles were driven past on their own missile launchers. There were fly-bys and battalions of infantry. The party leaders in their civilian coats and hats stood on the dark pink granite podium by Lenin's mausoleum and waved to the people, to the soldiers, to the children.

I took the metro to Ploshchad Ilyicha, and began walking. Everybody was going somewhere. Roads were barricaded off. Police hung around street corners, looking up and down without conviction. It was a real festive atmosphere, and I had my camera and was snapping away. I saw soldiers like I'd never seen before. They marched in ranks, and when they passed me all their heads turned at the same slow speed towards something, or somebody, further up the road beyond a stand that was selling ice cream. The black peaks on their caps gleamed, the bayonets attached to their rifles glinted in the sun.

I was trying to get to Red Square, but each time the roads were closed off, cordons were up, and policemen standing by. I managed to get close, but on the wrong side of the river. I could see the edge of the square and the massed crowds, but wasn't able to walk over the bridge. I thought I might be able to get round from another side, and retraced my steps until I found myself on a long, empty road.

It was midday. A tank turned a corner and headed straight for me. More came from behind, a vibrating line of darkness, each tank with its hatch open and a helmeted artilleryman carrying a rifle. They ran past at speed – there was nothing slow about them. The left track of the last tank clipped the side of a manhole cover and the iron-cast lid, heavy enough to break a person's legs, flipped up like a coin and began rolling down the street, veered to one side, hit the high curb and came to a crashing stop. The tanks were gone, leaving a stink of burnt fuel. The weather was perfect, cloudless and baking hot. I didn't realise – nobody did – that this was to be the last May Day parade in the Soviet Union, that the union would soon break up, that the whole idea of the socialist state which had banked so much trust, which had taken so many lives, and made so many millions of declarations and promises, would soon dissolve away into nothing, that it would leave without saying goodbye, without even a plausible explanation as to why it had stuck around for so long.

...

It's cool out. I make my way to Kuznetsky Most, through the heavy doors of the metro and down the escalator decorated with gilded flames to the underground concourse, a marble fantasy world like the insides of a marine creature, pink, white, smooth. It's busy down here, and has a musty smell. The faces around me look soft, pudgy, different from English faces.

There was a time when I was interested in 'the situation'. I liked to hear people define themselves and how things were in this country. They were all voices of people who had been disillusioned early in life and didn't want to fall into the same trap again, the innocent and not-so-innocent, those who wouldn't sign up to the party line and its double-standards. But whether those people really were innocent or not, guilty or not, didn't matter. When I looked through the apartment windows at the bricks laid so straight, the same in Moscow as anywhere else in the world, it seemed to me that these people's certainties dissolved away meaninglessly. The sameness of the bricks and the walls undermined idealism, the idealism of the West as well as the East. Men were flimsy because their works were so similar. But if men were flimsy, they were also stamped with an imprint of everything. They were like gods: there was nothing that wasn't theirs except for that one tiny thing, that detail, the joker in the pack that my father talked of, the thing that won't plop into place, the thing that is always there in the background, in the shadows behind you, or to the side of you. That thing that approaches in the end that you are scared of, or better say terrified of.

There is a roar and simultaneously an explosion of foul sweet-smelling air. The green train fills the platform and everybody prepares to push themselves on. There's something different in these people, a change in their style. They're less defiant than they used to appear. Their seriousness has been watered down.

They don't look quite European, but neither is there the absolute difference, the sharp division between peoples and continents that used to be so obvious.

The moment I stepped off the train at Belorussky vokzal thirty years ago has become distorted, but is still clear in my memory. The sun shone through carriages that stood taller than life and cast shadows like skyscrapers. The twin towers of the main building poked up from green and white striped walls. Outside the station, on the other side of the square, a white church was topped by a cluster of golden domes, like a clutch of newly-laid eggs. Trolley-buses moved through the streets. It was the moment I crossed from one world to another. The worlds existed side by side, but you couldn't hold onto both at the same time. Not then. It was either one or the other. West or East. Moscow or London.

Later on Russia crashed, and out of the destruction pieces of wreckage kept bobbing up and then disappearing again. Everything was topsy-turvy for a while, and in this twilight world the old intellectual guard made up their own vision. It was a perverse view in which Stalinist towers tilted at angles like cardboard cutouts, Gorbachev crawled on all fours around a drawing room floor wearing only a dog's studded collar, a chunk of uranium moved around the world in an attaché case, Nadezhda Mandelstam reclined on a daybed in a house-dress in a tiny apartment, her puffed-up body resembling one of Henri Rousseau's grotesque doll-like images, Gorky Street was swept with golden sunlight, a whole mass of pointless convictions webbed together to form something durable, a man with a smile thought he had found the answer to all things, two worlds met but did not mix, a poisonous scum drifted and couldn't be dealt with. It was a vision in which, once more, everybody was full of hate, nothing was what it seemed, and tyrants ruled the world.

The faces around me look uninterested, preoccupied, a little lumpen as if something had left them and was now out of reach forever. A song comes to me. A sad song of love. Love is painful. I could never understand that, but now I can. It's painful because there comes a point when it finishes, when it has to be cut away as a surgeon works on a diseased body to make it better. And then you have to remember the whole picture, because while you might be able to cut away at a body, and while this might be necessary to preserve its health, when it comes to the life you lead it's a different story. Your own life cannot be separated or divided into pieces. Just the opposite is true. It must be gathered up, assembled, made sense of.

Everywhere I go things have changed. Many places have been destroyed or else they have changed so much there is nothing left worth remembering. The brown building that has replaced Lyuba's old tenement seems to me like something from a different world. It will never be possible to walk through the blue-painted door to the line of holiday lets near the sea. But if I look at photos of myself standing in the full glare of sun on the beach I see the same uncertainty, the same crease in my forehead I always had. The smiles and easy gestures are overlaid onto it, but that thing which is me is still there, as if it could never be erased.

Yesterday a text came through from Daisy, a picture of the cranberry marsh in Vashutino. The picture shows her sitting on one of the soft mounds deep in the forest, holding a bucket with berries. She looks happy and wears a polka-dot bandana wrapped around a soft hat to protect her head from the ticks and mosquitoes. The bucket tilts forwards so you can see how many berries there are. Miles is not in the picture, and probably he didn't go. He doesn't like getting bitten, nor does he like walking much. But mainly he doesn't like picking berries, because it's such a dull occupation.

One of my ankles is aching, and the bottom of my back feels as if it needs straightening out. Probably I should find a place to stretch and do some yoga as Olga used to, before she discovered her Jewishness and got happy. For her, revelation turned out to be just another way of seeing, like going out of the back door instead of the front one. There had always been something out there, already written-down in fact, and it became a simple question of letting it into her life.

I hang onto the ceiling bar with one hand, taking the weight off my leg and easing myself into a better position, squashed by all these people, trying to think my way through all the deceptions. For the last time I make an effort to picture those things that seem important, or let's say long-lasting: to see the lines of red bricks that make up the mansion blocks, to remember the grotty smells, the broken stairwells, the wide avenues that in June were filled as in an old-fashioned ticker-tape parade with slow drifting poplar fluff, to hear the off-beat rhythm of the lambada coming from open windows in student halls, to remember the empty skies over the city on cool autumn evenings, the wet streets and steam rising from the cracked heating pipes, the snow, the rasping sound of a wood-framed window opening, the morning greeting, a barely audible whisper from crumpled sheets through a tangle of hair.

The train rushes into Taganskaya and for a moment the crowded platform flooded in a bright pool of light looks unrecognisable, as if I was seeing it all for the first time. Marble studded mosaics curl up each vaulted arch, pointed and deep blue, like dark trees marking the edge of a snowbound forest. From a niche between two pillars an alabaster bust of a beautiful young woman, surrounded by a halo of machine guns, turns towards the stairs with a look of faint boredom on her face. Then the doors shut, and the train moves out with steady controlled violence, back into the tunnel.

ABOUT THE AUTHOR

Stephen Morris was born in 1964. He went to school in Watford and later studied at The Royal Academy of Art.

He lives and works in London and Suffolk.

Black Tea is his first book.

If you enjoyed *Black Tea* then check out other great books from **Claret Press**.

Claret Press publishes political fiction and creative non-fiction. While all our books have a political edge, we mean politics in the widest meaning of the word, from the esoteric to the commercial. We love stories that introduce readers to new ideas, unexplored places and pivotal events both here in the UK and across the globe.

Claret Press books inform, engage and entertain.

To know more about our books, like us on Facebook or subscribe to our website **www.claretpress.com**

Lightning Source UK Ltd.
Milton Keynes UK
UKHW031045190922
409092UK00003B/486